EARTH SCIENCE

Lab Manual

Fourth Edition

Donald R. Congdon

bju press®

Greenville, South Carolina

The authors and the publisher have made every effort to ensure that the laboratory exercises in this publication are safe when conducted according to the instructions provided. We assume no responsibility for any injury or damage caused or sustained while performing activities in this book. Conventional and homeschool teachers, parents, and guardians should closely supervise students who perform the exercises in this manual. More specific safety information is contained in the Teacher's Edition of the Earth Science Lab Manual, Fourth Edition, published by BJU Press. Therefore, it is highly recommended that the Teacher's Edition be used in conjunction with this manual.

NOTE: The fact that materials produced by other publishers may be referred to in this volume does not constitute an endorsement of the content or theological position of materials produced by such publishers. Any references and ancillary materials are listed as an aid to the student or the teacher and in an attempt to maintain the accepted academic standards of the publishing industry.

Earth Science Lab Manual
Fourth Edition

Donald Congdon, MA
Terrance Egolf, CDR, USN (Retired)
Rachel Santopietro

Consultant
Rebecca Cecil, MEng, P.E.

Bible Integration
Bryan Smith, PhD
Brian Collins, PhD

Project Editor
Rick Vasso, MDiv

Concept Design
Drew Fields

Cover Design
Nathan Hutcheon

Page Design
John Cunningham
Linda Hastie

Project Coordinator
Donald Simmons

Photo Acquisition
Rita Mitchell
Kristin Villalba

Text Permissions
Sylvia Gass

Illustrators
Peter Crane
John Cunningham
Aaron Dickey
Terrance Egolf
Preston Gravely
James Hargis
Brian Johnson
Jonathan Johnson
Nathan Kirsop
Sarah Lyons
David Schuppert
Del Thompson

Formerly published as *Space and Earth Science*, 3rd Edition, by Terrance Egolf and Franklin Hall. First Edition by George Mulfinger Jr. and Donald Snyder. First published as *Earth Science for Christian Schools*.™

Photograph credits appear on page 245.
COVER: Photo and specimen: www.fabreminerals.com

© 2012 BJU Press
Greenville, South Carolina 29609

Third Edition © 2005 BJU Press
Second Edition © 1993, 1999 BJU Press
First Edition © 1986 BJU Press

Printed in the United States of America
All rights reserved

ISBN 978-1-60682-071-1

15 14 13 12 11 10 9 8 7 6

Contents

Becoming a Student Scientist

What do you think of when you think of a scientist? Maybe you think of a chemist in a lab, an oceanographer scuba-diving, a geologist collecting samples in the Grand Canyon, or an astronomer on a mountaintop looking through a huge telescope at a starry sky. One of the great things about science is that you don't just study it in the classroom. Science is a hands-on experience!

Much of that hands-on experience happens in science laboratories. But laboratories don't always look like they do on TV: you know, bubbling flasks full of colored liquids, Bunsen burners shooting tall yellow flames into the air, and an absent-minded scientist in a white lab coat and wearing thick glasses wandering around deep in thought.

Many laboratories aren't even inside a building. An earth scientist's laboratory may be floating on a bobbing boat, up high on a mountain, or deep in a cave. That's why earth science is so exciting.

This class can change you! Right now, you're a science student. But if you keep an open mind, along the way you'll be transformed into a student scientist. The key to becoming one is to learn to think and work like a real scientist does. That's what this book is all about.

Figure 1 Not all laboratories and scientists look like this!

Learning from the Laboratory

The laboratory is the place where classroom learning comes to life. Each lab activity in this book ties in with your textbook. But labs do more than just illustrate the science found in the textbook. They also teach you the skills that scientists need.

You'll learn to use scientific instruments, collect data, and make models. You'll read maps, access online resources, and perform chemical tests. These are things real scientists do every day.

Completing a Lab

When it's time to complete a lab, don't treat it like something to finish as fast as you can. Treat a lab as an opportunity to stretch yourself, like a good mental workout. *Think* about what you're doing. *Connect* it to the textbook chapter. *Sharpen* your science skills. And above all, *apply* what you discover as you answer the questions in each lab.

These questions aren't just busywork! They're designed to help you think deeply about science, just like real scientists do. Answer each question completely and thoroughly. Be sure to answer each part of the question.

Directions, Directions

Real scientists know that it's important to follow directions. Science works best when everything is organized and under control. Directions help scientists avoid making silly mistakes. They also help them reach reliable and useful conclusions.

So when you work through a lab, follow the directions carefully. *Read* each step. Be sure that it makes sense. *Ask* if you aren't certain about what you're supposed to do. *Measure* carefully. *Record* data accurately. And above all, *keep thinking!*

Worldview in the Laboratory

When professional scientists work in the laboratory, their worldviews always affect what they're doing. When they draw conclusions, their worldviews are hard at work. And their very reason for doing science comes from their worldviews.

As a student scientist, keep your worldview in mind too. When you do an experiment, think about how it relates to a biblical worldview. Some questions will ask you to apply your worldview to the problem. You always need to think like a Christian as you're doing science.

Staying Safe

Professional scientists are very serious about safety. No scientist wants to be killed, lose his eyesight, or experience painful injuries while doing an experiment. And no scientist wants to be responsible for injuring someone else when carrying out an experiment.

While the experiments that you'll be doing are designed to be safe, any experiment can injure you if you're not careful. Safety rules help to prevent accidents. But even more important than memorizing safety rules is learning to *think safe*. Think ahead and spot unsafe situations. In other words, *prevent* an injury before it happens. That's what professional scientists do. Let's explore some safety strategies.

Spotting Hazards

When you're in the laboratory, *keep your eyes open!* Look around for things that could cause injuries. These include objects that could trip someone, chemicals that could splatter, and heat sources that could burn.

Before using a sharp tool, think about what else it could cut besides what you're trying to cut. Are you protecting yourself, others, and the cutting surface?

You should also *keep your mind engaged.* Think about how something could break. Ask yourself, "What will happen if I do this or that? Will it fly off in a particular direction? Or will it suddenly become sharp? Is anyone standing in the line of fire?" Remember, you can't be thinking safe if you're messing around, talking, or daydreaming!

Poisons

Poisons aren't found just in murder mysteries. Many chemicals, including those under your kitchen sink, are poisonous. They may not kill you, but they can make you very sick. You won't be using

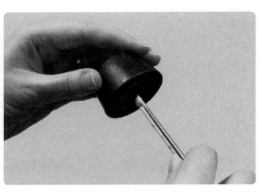
Figure 2 What could happen if the glass tube breaks?

anything very poisonous in these lab activities, but some chemicals could make you ill if you're not careful.

How can you protect yourself? Keep chemicals out of your body! Never taste a chemical. Eating or drinking while working with chemicals is obviously a very foolish idea. And eating or drinking after working with chemicals is also pretty risky. Always wash your hands after lab is over so you don't unintentionally eat a snack spiced with chemicals! Some chemicals can get into your body through the skin, so wash chemicals off your skin immediately.

Burns

Burns hurt! And most of the time they're easily preventable. Be alert for anything that gets hot. Burners, stoves, and open flames all present easy ways to get burned. Even more dangerous is hot glass. It looks cool, but it can be *very* hot! Whenever you're doing a lab that involves heat, keep asking yourself the question "Is this hot?" before you touch anything.

Chemicals can burn you too. Strong acids and bases attack your skin and eyes, causing pain and damage. If you ever come in contact with a strong acid or base, wash it off immediately with lots of running water. Laboratories usually have special stations to wash your eyes if chemicals get into them. Know where the eyewash station is in your lab.

Fire and Heat

When you're using heat, fire is always possible. Keep flammable things away from heat sources. Know where your laboratory fire extinguishers are, and know how to use them. Always follow your teacher's rules for fire prevention and evacuation.

Heat things carefully. Containers can crack if they're heated when almost empty. Keep open containers pointed away from you so you don't get a blast of hot steam in your face. Remember, microwave ovens can be dangerous too. They can make something just as hot as a stove or burner.

Field Work

When you're working out in the field, there are even more hazards. These include cars, places to fall, deep water, foul-smelling mud, snakes, hornets, poison ivy, and angry bulls. Your eyes are your best defense. Look before you leap, walk, or touch.

Angry Mothers

Not all hazards can injure you, but some can make your mother very angry! Protect your clothing in the laboratory. If you're painting a model rocket, make sure you don't paint your clothes as well. Glues don't come out of clothing very easily. Many chemicals can stain clothing, and a few can burn holes in it. Wear old clothing or use protective garments such as aprons.

Figure 3 Is the beaker hot? You can't tell just by looking.

Figure 4 Not a good thing to touch!

Safety Gear

Safety gear may seem unnecessary, but it serves an important purpose. So when you're told to wear goggles, protective clothing, or gloves, do it! Goggles may be hot and steamy, but they keep a lot of things out of your eyes. Having two working eyes for a lifetime is definitely worth a few minutes of discomfort!

Your lab instructions will warn you if protective gear is needed. But any time you think protective gear is a good idea, use it.

Your school lab will probably have other safety features too. These include first-aid kits, eyewash stations, fire extinguishers, and chemical safety data sheets. But your lab will definitely come with one very important safety feature—your teacher.

When in doubt, ask! If you are uncertain how to do something, ask. If something spills, tell your teacher. If you get cut or burned, ask your teacher what to do. And if you don't know whether or not you need to use safety gear, ask first.

The Adventure Begins

You have an exciting year ahead as you become a student scientist. Come to class each day looking forward to what you are going to learn. Approach each lab as a new adventure in the giant laboratory of earth science. Above all, come to class each day ready to honor your Creator by learning more about the marvelous world He has given you to explore!

Figure 5 Wearing goggles may be uncomfortable, but being blind is worse!

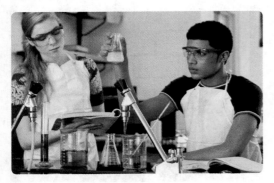

Figure 6 Could this be you?

1 THE WORLD OF EARTH SCIENCE

1A Feeding the World through Earth Science

name_____

section_____   date_____

Do you know how many people live in the world today? Almost 7 billion! Genesis 1:28 says that God told Adam and Eve to "be fruitful, and multiply, and replenish the earth, and subdue it." In other words, filling the earth and subduing it are connected. Some acts of dominion are not possible without an earth filled with humans. And, as we will see in this lab, some acts of dominion enable humans to fill the earth. How quickly did people fill the earth? Let's answer that question by building a model of the world's population for the last 2000 years.

> **Goals**
> After completing this lab, you will be able to
> ✓ create graphical models using supplied data.
> ✓ use your models to answer questions.
> ✓ evaluate possible causes and effects.
> ✓ discuss the role of science in fulfilling the Creation Mandate.

Procedure

- The chart below shows estimates of the world's population from AD 1 to 2000. Using the first graphing area on page 4, plot the population by finding the proper year on the *x*-axis and putting a dot at the correct place along the *y*-axis.

> **Equipment**
> graph paper (provided)

Year (AD)	Population (millions)
1	170
200	190
400	190
600	200
800	220
1000	265
1200	360
1400	350
1600	545
1800	900
2000	5750

Derived from http://en.wikipedia.org/wiki/World_.population_estimates (McEvedy column)

Figure 1 How large was the world's population at different points in history?

- Draw a smooth curve between the points. (Don't just connect the dots with straight lines.)

1. How can you tell by just looking at a graph whether something is changing quickly or slowly?

_____the lines_____

_____

2. Did the world's population grow quickly or slowly for most of the last 2000 years?

_____slowly_____

We call the steepness of a graph its *slope*. The steeper the slope, the faster the graph is changing. When scientists study something, they will often create a graph so they know how fast it's changing. Examining the graph's slope provides the answer.

3. When did the world's population suddenly start growing quickly?

_____1,800_____

_____

Your graph can't answer this question very well because there aren't enough data points to show you when the world's population started growing rapidly. Let's draw another graph to help narrow things down.

- The chart below shows estimates of the world's population from 1800 to 2000. Using the second graphing area on page 4, plot the population by finding the proper year on the *x*-axis and putting a dot at the correct place along the *y*-axis.

Year (AD)	Population (millions)	Year (AD)	Population (millions)
1800	980	1910	1753
1810	1045	1920	1888
1820	1069	1930	2073
1830	1138	1940	2299
1840	1192	1950	2528
1850	1244	1960	3035
1860	1270	1970	3696
1870	1309	1980	4442
1880	1397	1990	5279
1890	1516	2000	6085
1900	1633		

Derived from http://en.wikipedia.org/wiki/World_population_estimates (Hyde column)

- Draw a smooth curve between the points. (Don't just connect the dots with straight lines.)

4. What should you look for to decide when the world's population started growing rapidly?

_____

5. When did the world's population suddenly start growing very quickly?

_____1930's_____

In 1913, two chemists, Fritz Haber and Carl Bosch, introduced a method (the Haber-Bosch Process) to turn the nitrogen in the air into synthetic fertilizer. Suddenly it was possible to grow much larger quantities of food than ever before. Today, fertilizer made by the Haber-Bosch Process helps grow over one-third of the earth's food!

name_____

Figure 2 A Haber-Bosch synthetic ammonia plant

- Draw a vertical line on your graph through 1913.

6. Do you see a possible connection between the introduction of synthetic fertilizer and world population growth?

    yes. population started growing rapidly shortly
    after this event, so it could have been a contributing
    factor

7. What other factors besides synthetic fertilizer might have helped the world's population grow so quickly?

    medical care, agricultural, living,
    technological

8. Explain why the Haber-Bosch Process is an example of humans following God's command in Genesis 1:28.

    by enabling the land to provide more food, the
    human population can grow, and growth fulfills
    gods command to fill the RAther

9. Some think that today's world has too many people. From their point of view, the Haber-Bosch Process was a bad discovery. Do you agree? What do you think a person holding to the biblical worldview would say?

    no according to Genesis

10. During the past 200 years, many scientific discoveries have enabled the world's population to grow rapidly. If these discoveries had never been made, how many people do you think would be in the world today? Explore what might have happened by continuing the shape of your graph *before* 1913 up to 2000.

    we can not know for sure
    most likly less that 2.5 billion

World Population (AD 1 – 2000)

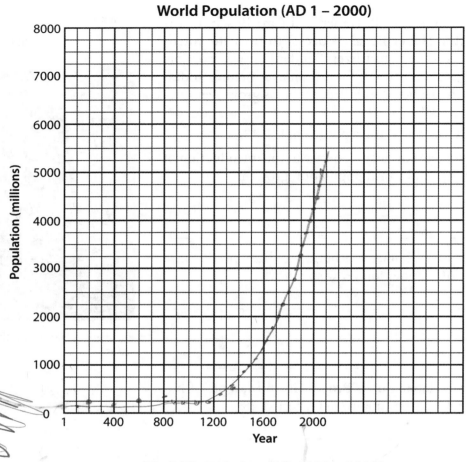

World Population (AD 1800 – 2000)

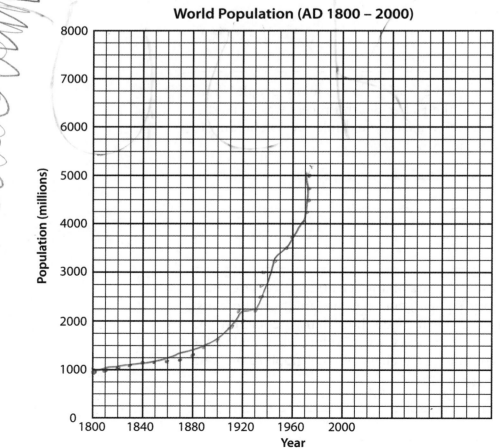

1B Finding the Standard Carrot

name _____

section _____ date _____

Scientists spend a lot of their time collecting *data*. Data can be numbers like weight, temperature, or length. It can also be a quality like color, luster, or shape. Scientists collect data by using their senses just like you do. They also use special instruments to examine what they are interested in. But real data isn't "perfect." Objects in the real world are almost never identical. So scientists often need to know the typical or average value for something. But how do we determine this value? Let's find out by determining the standard weight of a mini carrot.

Procedure

- Your teacher will give you twenty mini carrots. As you can see, they are similar but not identical. Using your laboratory scale, weigh each carrot and round its weight to the nearest 0.5 g. Your teacher will show you how to use the scale and round your numbers correctly. Record the weights in the first column of the table below.

Sample #	Weight (g)	Sorted Weight (g)
1		
2		
3		
4		
5		
6		
7		
8		
9		
10		
11		
12		
13		
14		
15		
16		
17		
18		
19		
20		

Goals

After completing this lab, you will be able to
- ✓ explain what a "standard" value is.
- ✓ describe the need for standard values.
- ✓ use a laboratory scale to collect data.
- ✓ sort and graph your data.
- ✓ use your graph to determine a "standard" value.

Equipment

mini carrots (20)
laboratory scale (accurate to 0.1 g)
graph paper (provided)

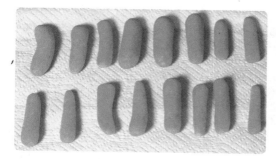

Figure 1 A collection of carrots

Figure 2 Collecting data

- Examine your data. The weights will probably vary by up to a few grams, but they should be similar. Some weights may be more common than others. But it's hard to tell what is typical just by looking at the numbers. We'll rearrange the data so it's easier to understand.

- Copy your data into the second column of the table, sorting it by weight. Put the smallest weight first, then the next smallest, and so on, until you finish with the largest weight.

- Most people understand data better if it's in picture form, so let's make a graph of our carrot weights.

- Look at the graphing area on the facing page. The *y*-axis represents the number of carrots with the same weight. The *x*-axis isn't scaled yet. Label the first box with the smallest weight found in your data. Label the next box with 0.5 g more than that weight. Keep going, adding 0.5 g to the previous weight until you reach the last weight found in your data.

- Now, go back to the first box on the *x*-axis. Shade in as many boxes as there are carrots with this weight. Move on to the next box and shade in as many boxes as there are carrots with that weight. Keep going until you've filled in boxes for each weight. If there are no carrots for a particular weight, don't shade any boxes for that weight.

- The graph you have just made is called a *histogram*. It's like a bar graph, but its purpose is to show which values are most common. In this case, it will help you decide the value of a "standard" carrot.

1. Which bar do you think represents the standard carrot weight? Why?

   _____

2. What could make the previous question difficult to answer?

   _____

3. If this situation happened, what could you do to solve the problem?

   _____

4. What do you conclude if all of your histogram's bars are approximately the same height?

   _____

   _____

   _____

name_____

Carrot Mass Histogram

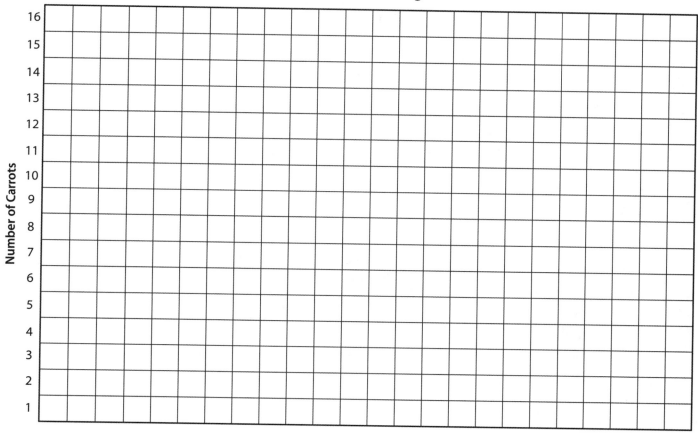

Number of Carrots

Mass (g)

1C Insufficient Data

name_____

section_____   date_____

Data is the raw material of science. No matter what a scientist studies, whether stars, rocks, animals, or a machine, he will describe it using data. Without data, scientists couldn't make *models*. Data comes from many places and has many forms. To understand scientific events and processes, you need data. But how much data do you need? Can you have too little? Let's model something using different amounts of data. We'll see what happens if we don't have enough.

Procedure

Imagine that you're a weather scientist studying how temperatures change. You decide to collect temperature data from two major cities: Phoenix, Arizona, and Boston, Massachusetts. Phoenix is a desert city, and Boston is a coastal city. You will collect data for a single day (24 hours), midnight to midnight.

You decide to collect temperatures every twelve hours, starting at midnight. You put the data into a table.

Time	Phoenix (°C)	Boston (°C)
0000 (midnight)	32	19
1200 (noon)	37	29
2400 (midnight)	33	22

- Plot the data on the first graphing area on page 12. Use two different colors so you can tell the cities apart. Draw short colored lines and write each city name in the legend box in the upper right corner. Draw straight lines between the points. We'll call this graph "Model 1."

Your graph is a model of daily temperature change for the two cities. Models are supposed to represent what actually happened. So, in theory, you can use a model to give you numbers that aren't in the original data.

1. What do you think Phoenix's temperature was at 9:00 AM (0900)?

_____

2. What was Boston's temperature at 3:00 PM (1500)?

_____

3. Are you confident that this model accurately represents the temperatures of these two cities? Why or why not?

_____

_____

Goals

After completing this lab, you will be able to
- ✓ graph data to reveal trends.
- ✓ describe how insufficient data can lead to poor models.
- ✓ explain the need for "enough" data.

Equipment

graph paper (provided)
colored pens or pencils

Figure 1 Phoenix (top) and Boston (bottom) are located in significantly different climates.

Adding more data may improve our model. Let's collect temperatures every four hours and see what happens.

Time	Phoenix (°C)	Boston (°C)
0000 (midnight)	32	19
0400	27	19
0800	28	23
1200 (noon)	37	29
1600	39	29
2000	38	26
2400 (midnight)	33	22

- Plot the data on the Model 2 graphing area on page 12. Use two different colors so you can tell the cities apart. Create a legend in the legend box. Draw straight lines between the points.

4. What do you think Phoenix's temperature was at 9:00 AM (0900)?

_____

5. What was Boston's temperature at 3:00 PM (1500)?

_____

6. Are you confident that this model accurately represents the temperatures of these two cities? Why or why not?

_____

_____

Let's add some more data. We'll collect temperatures every hour.

Time	Phoenix (°C)	Boston (°C)
0000 (midnight)	32	19
0100	32	19
0200	29	20
0300	29	20
0400	27	19
0500	27	19
0600	26	20
0700	27	22
0800	28	23
0900	31	24
1000	32	26
1100	34	27
1200 (noon)	37	29

Time	Phoenix (°C)	Boston (°C)
1300	37	31
1400	37	32
1500	38	31
1600	39	29
1700	39	28
1800	39	23
1900	38	23
2000	38	26
2100	37	25
2200	33	25
2300	33	22
2400 (midnight)	33	22

- Plot the data on the Model 3 graphing area on page 13. Use two different colors so you can tell the cities apart. Create a legend in the legend box. Draw straight lines between the points.

name_____

7. What do you think Phoenix's temperature was at 9:00 AM (0900)?

_____

_____

8. What was Boston's temperature at 3:00 PM (1500)?

_____

_____

9. Are you confident that this model accurately represents the temperatures of these two cities? Why or why not?

_____

_____

_____

10. Now go back and compare your three sets of answers. How good was Model 1? Model 2?

_____

_____

_____

Scientists often look at graphs to identify *trends*. A trend is the general direction that the data seems to be going.

11. Look at all three graphs of Boston's temperatures. Do you see any trends that one or more of the graphs misses?

_____

_____

_____

12. What have you learned about the importance of having enough data?

_____

_____

_____

Scientists use historical temperature data to model the climate so they can predict future temperatures. However, we don't have many instrument-based temperature observations before 1850.

13. What is a possible problem with predicting future climate from models created with limited historical temperature data?

_____

_____

_____

_____

Model 1

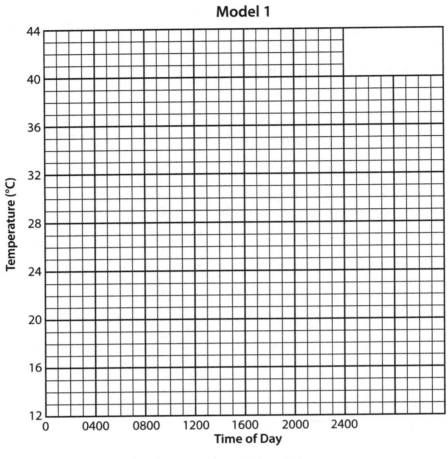

Model 2

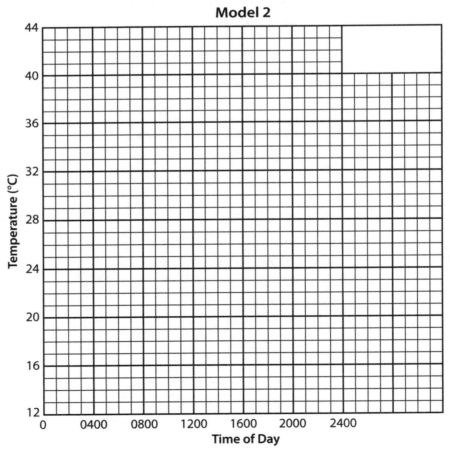

Model 3

name _____

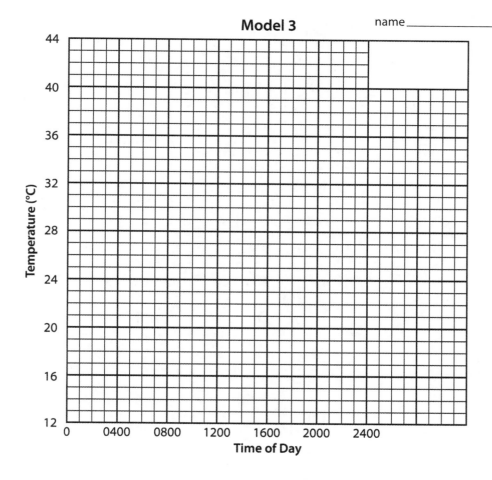

2 MATTER, FORCES, AND ENERGY

2A Measuring Matter

name _____

section _____   date _____

Oak and pine are both types of wood, but you'd never mistake one for the other. What makes them different? You might say color, grain, or even odor. But once you pick up identically sized pieces of each, you'll notice something important. The oak feels a lot heavier than the pine. What quality makes oak heavier? This quality also makes oak harder and stronger than pine. In fact, this property largely determines what the wood is good for. But what is this mysterious property called? Let's find out!

Procedure

- Your teacher has given you four blocks of wood, all about the same size. Record the type of wood in the "Sample" columns of the two tables on the next page.

- Take a moment to handle each block. How heavy does it feel? How hard or soft? Does any particular quality jump out at you? Write it down in the "Observations" column.

You've just collected what scientists call *descriptive data*. Descriptive data is a record of impressions, usually collected by the senses. This kind of data can be useful, but it has one big problem.

1. What is descriptive data's big weakness?

_____

_____

_____

Scientists usually prefer *measured data*. Measured data takes the form of numbers and often comes from instruments, so it's consistent. It also isn't as easily influenced by people's opinions because everyone is comparing the measured object to the same standard. Different observers using the same instrument should get the same result. Let's collect some measured data from our wood blocks.

- Measure the mass of each sample using the laboratory scale. Round the mass to the nearest 0.1 g and record it in the "Mass" column of both tables.

- Measure the length, width, and height of the sample using the ruler. Record each measurement, rounded to the nearest 0.1 cm (1 mm), in the appropriate column.

Goals

After completing this lab, you will be able to

✓ contrast descriptive and measured data.

✓ use laboratory tools to collect data.

✓ use data to create new data.

✓ define density and explain how it's measured in solids.

✓ predict a material's behavior based upon its density.

Equipment

wood block samples (4)
laboratory scale (accurate to 0.1 g)
centimeter ruler

Figure 1 What color is this block of bloodwood? Red? Orange? Brownish-red? It's subjective!

Sample	Observations	Mass (g)	l (cm)	w (cm)	h (cm)

Figure 2 Collecting measured data

- You probably remember from math class that the word *volume* refers to the space something takes up. Let's find the volume of each block.

2. How do you calculate the volume of a box?

_____

3. What is the proper unit for volume if your size measurements are all in centimeters?

_____

- Calculate the volume of each block and record it in the "Volume" column of the table below. Include the proper units and round each result to one decimal place.

- We've already noticed that different woods with the same volume can have different masses. We're going to link these quantities together by creating a ratio of mass to volume.

- Determine the mass-to-volume ratio by dividing the mass by the volume. Record your answers in the "Ratio" column. Round each result to two decimal places.

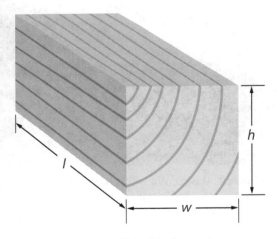

Figure 3 The wood block's dimensions

Sample	Mass (g)	Volume	Ratio

4. What do you notice about the ratios and your descriptive data from the blocks?

_____

_____

- Although you may not know it yet, your ratio is an important property of matter called *density*. A dense object is heavier than another identical object made of a less dense material.

- We need to know one more thing before we're finished. What is the unit for density? Think of the units used in our ratio. We used mass (g) and volume (cm^3).

5. How should we combine these units to get the unit for density?

name_____

_____

You've already seen simple units like grams, centimeters, and °C before. But you may have never seen a unit that is made up of other units. Science has lots of these. They're called *derived units*.

• Now that you know the proper unit for density, write the units next to the density values in the "Ratio" column.

You've just done something important with your data. You've created new data from the old. You now know the density value for each type of wood. Scientists often create new data by performing calculations on old.

Woods have different densities because their cell structures are different. The chemicals that make up the cell walls also vary among wood types. Density is very important because it determines what the wood can do. Dense woods can be very hard, but they are often brittle. Less dense woods are lighter, more flexible, and often float well. Scientists and engineers need to learn about the properties of matter so they can use them to fulfill God's command to have dominion over the earth.

6. Which do you think would float better, oak (high density) or balsa (low density)? Why?

_____

_____

7. Which would make a better tabletop? Why?

_____

_____

_____

8. White oak has a typical density of 0.71 g/cm³, while white spruce has a typical density of 0.41 g/cm³. If you were building an airplane wing, which one would be a better choice? Why?

_____

_____

_____

9. Balsa has a typical density of 0.16 g/cm³. If a balsa log has a volume of 105,000 cm³, do you think you could lift it? Explain why or why not.

_____

_____

Figure 4 Can you lift the log?

10. Could you lift a white oak log with the same volume? Explain why or why not.

   _____

   _____

2B Cooling Down

name_____

section_____   date_____

In Lab 2A, you learned about a property of solid matter called *density*. Density is the ratio of a substance's mass to its volume. Liquids have density too! But you can't measure a liquid's volume with a ruler. We'll have to do something a little different. Let's see how to find a liquid's density.

Procedure

- Place a dry, empty graduated cylinder on the laboratory scale. Measure its mass to the nearest 0.1 g. Record the mass in the table below.

- Carefully fill the graduated cylinder with 20 mL of distilled water. The top of the liquid curves in the cylinder. Fill it so that the bottom of the curve just touches the 20 mL mark. Be as exact as you can and use the eyedropper or pipette to "tweak" the amount to 20 mL.

- Place the filled cylinder on the laboratory scale. Measure its mass to the nearest 0.1 g. Record the mass in the table below.

1. You need to know the mass of the water only. What must you do?

_____

_____

- Calculate the mass of the water. Record it in the table below.

2. You know the volume of the water (20 mL), and you measured the mass of the liquid. How do you calculate the density of water?

_____

- Calculate the density of the water and record it, rounded to two decimal places, in the table below. (*Hint*: 1 mL = 1 cm^3.)

- Repeat the process with glycerin and canola oil. Use a clean graduated cylinder for each. Record the results in the table below.

Goals

After completing this lab, you will be able to

✓ determine the density of liquids.

✓ measure how liquids change when they freeze.

✓ determine the density of frozen liquids.

✓ identify a unique liquid.

Equipment

plastic graduated cylinders, 25 mL (3)
eyedropper or pipette
laboratory scale (accurate to 0.1 g)
freezer
distilled water
glycerin
canola oil

Figure 1 Measuring the liquid's mass

Liquid	Empty Mass (g)	Full Mass (g)	Liquid Mass (g)	Density (g/cm³)
water				
glycerin				
canola oil				

Does anything happen to a liquid's density when it freezes? In Chapter 2 of your textbook, you learned that matter is made of constantly moving particles. What happens to the particles when you cool them? They slow down and move closer together. If you cool a liquid enough, its particles lock into fixed patterns, and the liquid becomes a solid. These particles still move even when they're locked in a solid. We call this change *freezing*.

3. If a liquid's particles move closer together as it cools, what do you think happens to its volume when it freezes?

_____

_____

_____

4. Will a liquid's mass change when it freezes? Explain why or why not?

_____

_____

5. What do you think happens to a liquid's density when it freezes?

_____

_____

_____

- Let's test your idea by freezing the three liquids that you've just measured. Put the cylinders in a freezer. Leave them there overnight until they freeze solid.

- When the liquids are all frozen, remove the cylinders. Quickly find their volumes by reading the graduated cylinders' scales. Record the volumes in the table below.

- Calculate the frozen liquids' densities using the new volumes. Their masses haven't changed, so you can use the original mass values. Record the densities, rounded to two decimal places, in the table below.

Liquid	Solid Volume (cm³)	Solid Density (g/cm³)
water		
glycerin		
canola oil		

Figure 2 How does cooling change the liquids?

6. Was your prediction about frozen density correct? If not, what went wrong?

name_____

_____

_____

_____

Figure 3 Water is a special liquid.

In general, liquids shrink when they cool. Their volumes become smaller so their densities become greater. Water does the opposite, which is very unusual. In fact, hardly any other room-temperature liquids expand when they freeze.

7. Why is water's unusual behavior beneficial for life on Earth? (*Hint*: If ice is less dense than liquid water, will ice float or sink? What would happen to bodies of water if ice were denser than liquid water?)

_____

_____

_____

Optional Activity

Scientists have measured the densities of many liquids very accurately. We call these super-accurate numbers *accepted values*. When you determine a value by doing an experiment, it's called an *experimental value*. We often test the accuracy of our experiments by comparing experimental values to accepted values.

8. What could cause your experimental values to differ from the accepted values?

_____

_____

How close did your density values come to the accepted values? To compare an experimental value to an accepted one, scientists calculate what is called the *percent error*. They calculate percent error with the following formula:

$$\% \text{ error} = \frac{|\text{Accepted} - \text{Experimental}|}{\text{Accepted}} \times 100\%.$$

- The table on the next page shows the accepted values for the three liquids that you tested. Calculate the percent error for each of your unfrozen densities. Record the results, rounded to one decimal place, in the table.

Liquid	Accepted Density (g/cm³)	Percent Error (%)
water	1.0	
glycerin	1.3	
canola oil	0.9	

All experiments have some amount of error. So you shouldn't be surprised or alarmed if your percent error isn't zero. How much error is acceptable depends upon what you're doing. Percent errors of 5–10% are typical and just fine for most of the labs you'll be doing.

9. Do you think measuring density might be a good way to identify an unknown liquid? Why or why not?

_____

_____

_____

_____

3 MAPS AND MAPPING

3A Where Am I?

Knowing where you are on the earth hasn't always been easy. Genesis 1:14 tells us that there are markers in the heavens to help us exercise dominion. But it took thousands of years to figure out how these markers worked. While most people today use tools like GPS to navigate, we're going to find our latitude using the stars. This technique is called *celestial navigation.*

As you learned from your textbook, latitude is your position north or south of the Equator. One easy way to find your latitude is to use the pole star. A pole star appears to be directly above the north or south geographic pole. All the other stars in the sky appear to rotate around the pole star, which remains still. Polaris is the Northern Hemisphere's pole star. Sigma Octantis, a hard-to-see star, is the same for the Southern Hemisphere. You can see it only when you're south of the Equator.

1. If you were standing on the North Pole (lat. 90°N), where would you expect Polaris to be in the sky?

   _____

2. If you started moving south, what would Polaris appear to do?

   _____

3. If you were standing at the Equator (lat. 0°), where would you expect Polaris to be in the sky?

   _____

4. What is the connection between your latitude and the position of the pole star?

   _____

To find our latitude, we need to build a simple instrument to help us measure angles.

Procedure

- Thread the string through the hole drilled in the middle of the protractor's flat side and tie a knot. If there is no hole, tape it in place. Tie the weight to the other end of the string. Tape the straw to the protractor's flat side. You have just built a *clinometer,* a tool to measure angles.

- Let's practice before it gets dark. Go outside and find a tall object like a telephone pole. Look through the straw and tilt the protractor until you see the top of the pole.

- Have a partner look at the string, which should be hanging straight down. Read the angle number that the string passes

name _____

section _____ date _____

Goals

After completing this lab, you will be able to

✓ explain the relationship between the pole star's angle and latitude.

✓ locate the pole star.

✓ measure the angle of the pole star above the horizon.

✓ use the angle of the pole star to find your latitude.

Equipment

protractor
string or thread, 40 cm
weight (large nut or fishing sinker)
large diameter drinking straw

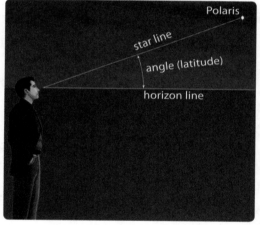

Figure 1 The pole star's angle above the horizon

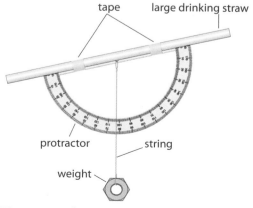

Figure 2 A clinometer

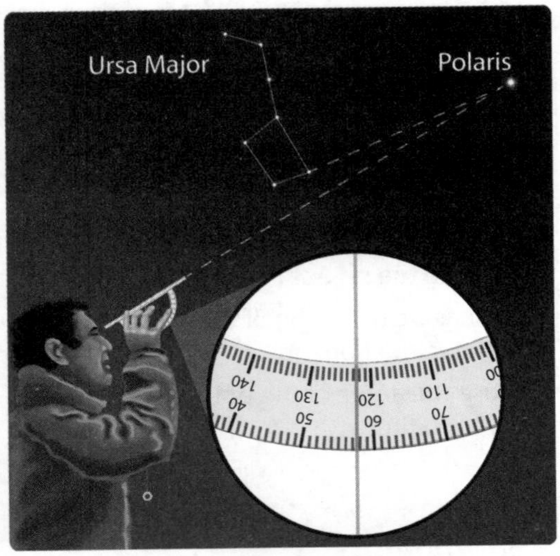

Figure 3 Measuring your latitude

through. If the protractor has two sets of numbers, use the number that is between 0 and 90.

- Subtract this number from 90.° The answer is the angle formed between the top of the pole and the horizon.

- Wait for it to get dark. Go outside and let your eyes adjust to the darkness for a few minutes. Then find the Big Dipper (Ursa Major).

- Once you've found the Big Dipper, sight along the two stars that make up the front of the bowl. You'll see a bright star at the end of the imaginary line that passes through these two stars. The bright star is Polaris, the Northern Hemisphere's pole star.

- Look through the clinometer's straw and tilt the protractor until you see Polaris. Have a partner read the number that the string passes through. Record it below.

_____

- Subtract this number from 90.° The answer is your latitude. Record it below.

_____

- Now, let's see how close you came to your actual latitude. Look up your actual latitude by using an online map, GPS, or other tool. Round the latitude to the nearest degree and record it below.

_____

5. How close was your measured latitude to the actual?

_____

_____

6. Can you think of reasons why your measured latitude might be different from the actual?

_____

_____

7. In a few sentences, briefly discuss why knowing your location is important for exercising wise dominion.

_____

_____

_____

_____

3B Measuring the Earth

name _____

section _____   date _____

If someone asked you to measure the earth's circumference, how would you do it? No tape measure would be long enough! Since scientists can't measure some things directly, they often have to do it *indirectly*. Eratosthenes, a Greek mathematician and astronomer (276–194 BC), devised a way to indirectly measure the distance around the earth.

Eratosthenes found that the sun cast no shadows at noon on the summer solstice (June 21) in the Egyptian city of Syene (modern Aswan). At the same time, a vertical object in the city of Alexandria cast a shadow with an angle of 7.2.° Alexandria was 5000 stadia (1 stadion = 185 m) almost directly north of Syene.

Eratosthenes believed, as did most Greek philosophers at the time, that the earth was a perfect sphere. By setting up a proportion, he calculated the polar circumference of the earth. We will use his method to measure the circumference of a desk globe.

Procedure

- In a darkened room, position the lamp at least 4 m away from the globe. At this distance the light rays are nearly parallel.

- Slowly move the first stick up and down along a longitude (vertical) line, keeping it perpendicular to the surface of the globe. Stop when it reaches the point where it casts no shadow. Fasten the stick onto the globe with a piece of clay.

- Confirm that the stick is perpendicular to the globe's surface by using the protractor. Place the protractor's straight edge on the globe and position it so that the globe's surface curves

Goals

After completing this lab, you will be able to

✓ explain why scientists sometimes must use indirect measurement methods.

✓ use Eratosthenes's method to measure the circumference of a globe.

Equipment

globe at least 20 cm in diameter (a large sports ball can be substituted)
spotlight or overhead projector
protractor
cloth centimeter tape measure
two sticks 2 mm thick and at least 10 cm long
string or thread
modeling clay

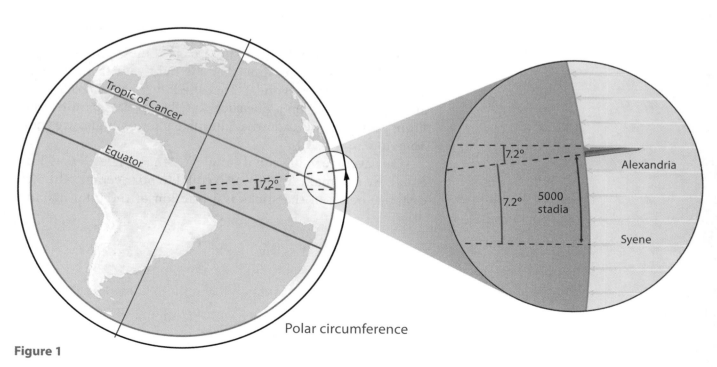

Figure 1

away equally on both sides of the point of contact. The stick should align with the 90° mark. Make this check parallel to both the longitude and latitude lines.

After completing this step, do not move the globe, or your results will be incorrect!

- Measure 5 cm directly north from the base of the stick. Using clay, fasten the second stick at that point. Use the protractor to make this stick perpendicular to the globe's surface.

- The second stick should be casting a shadow on the globe. Fasten one end of the string down with clay at the very tip of the shadow. Carefully, without moving the second stick, draw the string tight between the end of the shadow and the top of the second stick.

- Using the protractor, measure the angle formed between the second stick and the string. You may want someone to hold the string in place and keep the stick perpendicular to the globe as you do this. Record the angle in the table below.

- To improve your accuracy, repeat the measurement two more times. Record the results in the table.

- Average the three measurements and record the average in the table.

Measurement	Angle (°)
1	
2	
3	
Average	

Refer to Figure 2 on the next page. Lines *AB* and *CD* are parallel because we assume that the light rays from the lamp are parallel. Angles *X* and *Y* are called *alternate interior angles* and are formed when a line such as *CB* intersects parallel lines. From geometry, we know that alternate interior angles are equal. Therefore, $\angle X = \angle Y$.

Our average value equals angle *X*. Since angles *X* and *Y* are equal, we can make angle *Y* also equal to our average. The 5 cm distance between the sticks is a fraction of the total distance around the globe (the circumference). Since the circumference is a circle, it contains 360.° So we can create a proportion between distances and angles:

name _____

$$\frac{\text{circumference (cm)}}{5 \text{ cm}} = \frac{360°}{\angle Y}.$$

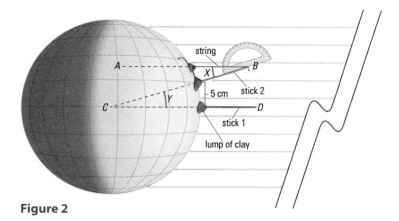

Figure 2

- Solve for the circumference of the globe. Record it below.

_____

- Now, let's measure the globe's actual circumference so we can check our indirect measurement. Wrap the cloth measuring tape around the globe from pole to pole. Make sure the tape follows a line of longitude. Record the circumference in centimeters below.

_____

- Let's see how close our indirect measurement came to the actual value. Calculate the percent error using the formula that you used in Lab 2B. Record your result below.

_____

1. Using Eratosthenes's data (given in the introduction to this lab), calculate the polar circumference of the earth in kilometers.

_____

2. The earth's accepted polar circumference is 40,009 km. Calculate Eratosthenes's percent error. Record it below.

_____

3. What are some possible sources of error in Eratosthenes's value for the earth's polar circumference?

_____

_____

_____

_____

4. The earth's circumference at the Equator is 40,075 km. Why is the equatorial circumference larger than the polar?

_____

_____

_____

3C The Best Vacation

name_____

section_____   date_____

What makes the difference between a good vacation and a disaster? Planning! A well-planned vacation makes good use of time. A poorly planned one is chaotic and frustrating. Planning a trip *before* you leave home is the key to having the best possible experience.

Deciding what to do and where to go couldn't be easier these days thanks to Geographic Information Systems, or GIS. Most GIS services are computer based. They combine maps and layers of useful information so you can explore geography in many different ways.

For example, let's say you wish to visit several historic landmarks. A GIS tool not only shows you the roads to take, but also shows you restaurants, gas stations, and other local attractions. GIS helps you measure the distances between landmarks. And GIS can show you pictures of the landmarks along with interesting information. Let's learn to use a popular GIS program called Google Earth.™ This program will be your virtual airplane and submarine as you explore earth science this year.

Goals

After completing this lab, you will be able to

✓ use the major features of a popular GIS tool.

✓ plan a vacation using a GIS tool.

Equipment

computer with Google Earth™

Procedure 1 (Using Google Earth™)

- Start Google Earth.™ You're looking at the earth from far out in space. We need to move in for a closer look.

- Look at the left side of the screen. Find the list marked **Layers**. Make sure every checkbox under this heading is unchecked.

- Now look near the top of the screen and find the box labeled **Fly to**. Type in **New York City, NY**, and hit **Enter**. Enjoy the ride as the program flies you to New York City!

- Since you didn't specify an exact location within New York City, Google Earth™ leaves you hovering over the center of the city. In this case, the center is Manhattan Island, seen from about 20 mi (32 km) up.

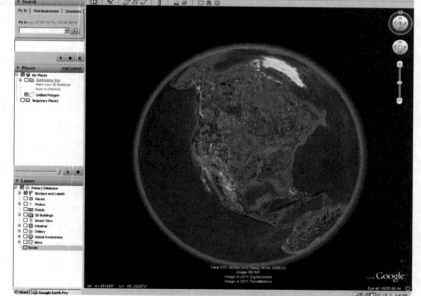

Figure 1

Data SIO, NOAA, U.S. Navy, NGA, GEBCO/Image IBCAO/ Image © 2011 DigitalGlobe/Image © 2011 TerraMetrics

- Zoom in a bit by rolling the mouse wheel. You can see your altitude by looking at **Eye alt** in the lower right corner of the screen. Zoom in until you're 8000–10,000 ft (2.4–3.0 km) up.

You're looking at high-resolution satellite images of the buildings and streets. In fact, if you zoom in close enough, you can even see cars and people!

Figure 2 Does this look familiar?

Keyboard Alternative

If you don't have a mouse with a wheel, you can tilt the perspective by holding down the **Shift** key and using the **Up** and **Down** arrow keys.

Figure 3 Central Park is a popular place for joggers.

- Move around by left-clicking the mouse and dragging. Spend a few minutes moving around and zooming in and out.
- Let's go somewhere specific. Type the following address in the **Fly to** box: **350 5th Ave., New York, NY**. Hit **Enter**. When you arrive, zoom in a bit.

1. Do you know what you're looking at?

_____

- Click the mouse wheel button and drag the mouse. You can tilt your viewpoint so you are no longer looking from above. Tilt the view so the world is almost flat.

2. What happens to the buildings?

_____

Remember, the images you're seeing are photos taken from space. There isn't much depth information available in satellite images. Many people have contributed digital models of major landmarks to Google Earth.™ The models are three-dimensional and greatly enhance the view.

- Tilt the world so it's no longer flat (about 45° works well). Zoom back to about 1500 ft (457 m). Look at the left side of the screen. Find the list marked **Layers**. Check the checkbox labeled **3D Buildings**.

3. What happens to the buildings?

_____

_____

- Uncheck the **3D Buildings** checkbox. Tilt the world so it's flat again. Check the **Roads** checkbox. Zoom in and out and move around.

4. What happens when you check this box?

_____

_____

When people vacation, they need to know distances so they can plan their transportation. Google Earth™ has several powerful measuring tools that can help with this.

- Zoom out so you can see all of Manhattan Island. Central Park is the big green rectangle in the middle of the island. Adjust the zoom level so you can see the whole park.
- Look at the toolbar below the menus. Find the tool that looks like a ruler and click it. The **Ruler** box will appear. Click the **Line** tab so it comes to the front.
- Left-click the bottom of Central Park. Left-click the top. A line will appear representing the distance across the park.

5. How long is Central Park in miles? in kilometers?

name _____

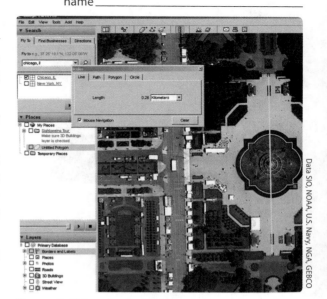

- Look at the middle of the park. A jogging path surrounds the large body of water (known as "the Reservoir"). But how long is the path?

- Zoom in so the Reservoir fills the screen. Select the **Ruler** tool and click the **Path** tab so it comes to the front.

- Left-click the mouse on an edge of the Reservoir. A dot appears. Click again a short distance away. Another dot appears, connected to the first by a line. Repeat this process until you've outlined the Reservoir as accurately as possible.

6. How long is the jogging path around the Reservoir in miles? in kilometers?

Figure 4 Using the **Ruler Line** tool

Vacationers want to know where to eat, where to stay, and what other attractions are in the area. GIS tools provide this information through *thematic layers* that appear on top of the map.

- Find the **Layers** list at the left side of the screen. Check the **Border and Labels** checkbox. Expand the **More** checkbox and check **Local Place Names**, **Parks/Recreation Areas**, and **Place Categories**. Many little symbols (icons) will appear, identifying different themes. For example, a knife and fork identifies a restaurant. A bed identifies a hotel. Click on a symbol to see what it represents.

- Spend a few minutes navigating around New York City. Look at the 3D buildings and landmarks. Examine the different thematic resources. Measure a few distances. And don't forget to check out the Statue of Liberty in 3D!

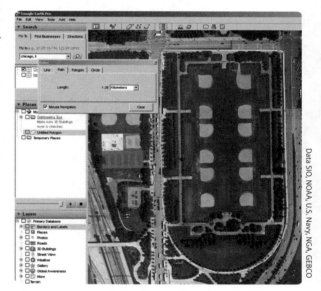

Figure 5 Using the **Ruler Path** tool

Procedure 2 (Planning a Vacation)

Now that you're a GIS expert, it's time to plan a vacation! The first thing to do is choose a city to visit. Assume that you have two days and that you'll be dropped off each day and travel on foot to each site.

- Choose a city that interests you and that has a large number of tourist sites. Students in the United States might want to visit Washington DC. Students living in other nations should select a major city either in their own country or in a country of interest.

1. Which city did you select?

Figure 6 The Statue of Liberty is a major symbol of New York City.

Figure 7 Washington DC is a popular vacation destination for many Americans.

- Spend a few minutes brainstorming for places to visit. Make a list of sites you'd like to see. Many vacationers have no idea how far apart sites are. Google Earth™ can help you create a realistic itinerary. Record your ideas in the table below.

- Now, start up Google Earth™ and **Fly to** your vacation city. Turn on the appropriate thematic layers (avoid **3D Buildings** at this point).

- Locate each site and do some measurements to see how far apart they are. Remember, you'll be traveling on foot!

- Create a chart for each day's itinerary. List each site. Estimate how much time you plan to spend there. Estimate travel time between each site by measuring the distance. While many people can walk 2–4 mi/h (3.2–6.4 km/h), the average tourist walks at a slower pace.

- Don't forget to eat! Select a suitable restaurant for lunch and for a mid-morning or afternoon break.

- See if you can find interesting things to see as you go from one site to the next. A brief stop near a significant landmark is fun and worthwhile.

- See if any of the major sites you plan to visit have 3D models available. Spend a few moments looking at the site in 3D.

3D What Time Is It?

name_____

section_____   date_____

We are time-based creatures. People often say that the clock runs their lives. In our modern world, clocks certainly play a big role. Clocks tell us when to get up, when to sleep, and when to go to work or school. Knowing the time, however, isn't as simple as it looks. People in ancient times didn't have the kinds of clocks we use. Let's see how they handled time. And let's see how we handle it now.

Procedure 1 (Ancient Time)

In the Bible the word *day* is used in at least two different ways. References like Genesis 1:5, in which God declares that "the evening and the morning were the first day," refer to a 24-hour period (one earth rotation). The Jewish day extended from sunset to sunset. The Roman day extended from midnight to midnight.

Another use of the word refers to the period from sunrise to sunset (approximately 12 hours). Our Lord Himself used this form in John 11:9: "Jesus answered, 'Are there not twelve hours in the day? If any man walk in the day, he stumbleth not, because he seeth the light of this world.'" Interestingly, this is the first direct mention of the 12-hour daylight period in the Bible.

In early Old Testament times, we find no evidence that the day was divided into numbered hours. They really didn't need to know the time in hours and minutes to do the things they did every day. Instead, terms such as sunrise, morning, noon, heat of the day, cool of the day, sunset, and evening were used.

In later Old Testament times, there is some evidence that time was divided into units. God's miracle of the shadow moving backward by ten units (2 Kings 20:9–11) suggests a numbered division of time. Beginning in the book of Matthew, there are references to "the third hour" of the day, "the sixth hour" of the day, and so forth.

The length of the daylight period varies with the latitude of the observer and the time of year. But we can assume that sunrise in the Scriptures means 6:00 AM and sunset means 6:00 PM. We can also assume that the hours have the same length as modern ones.

- Look up the time mentioned in each Bible reference listed in the table on the next page and record it in the middle column. Then calculate and record the modern clock time for each biblical time. Be sure to indicate whether it is am, pm, or noon. (*Hint:* Begin at 6:00 AM and count forward the given number of hours. For example, the fourth hour of the day would be 10:00 AM.) Note that the examples given are all from the New Testament.

Goals
After completing this lab, you will be able to
✓ define what the word *day* means in the Bible.
✓ convert times mentioned in the Bible to modern clock time.
✓ explain the reason for time zones.
✓ convert time between zones.

Equipment
none

Reference	Biblical Time	Modern Equivalent
Matthew 20:3		
Matthew 20:6		
Mark 15:33		
Mark 15:34		
John 1:39		
John 4:6		
John 4:52		
Acts 2:15		
Acts 3:1		
Acts 10:9		

Notice that this exercise deals with the daylight hours only. The night, from 6:00 PM to 6:00 AM, was divided into *watches*. In New Testament times there were four watches, each three hours in length. The night could also be subdivided into hours. Acts 23:23 refers to "the third hour of the night," corresponding roughly to 9:00 PM.

1. Give the two definitions of the word *day* in the Bible, both of them referring to a definite unit of time.

_____

_____

_____

2. In New Testament times, how many watches were there in a night?

_____

3. What is the modern clock time equivalent of the fourth watch?

_____

Procedure 2 (Modern Time)

In a modern society with flights to catch, appointments to keep, and schedules to coordinate in multiple countries, knowing just the local time isn't good enough. We apply technology to help us use God's world better.

Since the earth turns on its axis 15° per hour, astronomers and geographers have chosen to divide the earth into time zones that are each 15° of longitude wide. The 15° width of each zone allows the 360° of the globe to be evenly divided into 24 time zones.

name_____

Time zones are important so that everyone's clock time corresponds fairly closely to the sun's path across the sky. It's also important to note that all geographical points within a given zone share the same clock time.

The time zone system is centered on the *Prime Meridian*, the line of longitude running through Greenwich, England (the dotted line in Figure 1). In general, the time in each zone is one hour later than the time zone to its west. The one exception to this rule occurs at the International Date Line (in Figure 1, the dotted line located on the side of the earth farthest from the Prime Meridian). The date line splits the time zone into two 7½°-wide zones. Both sides of the date line have the same clock time but different dates. To the east of the date line, the date is one day earlier than it is to the west of

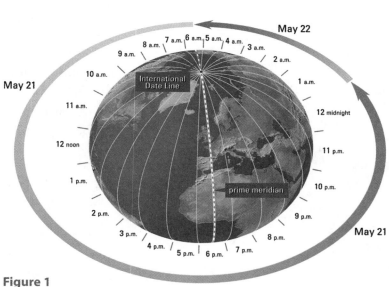

Figure 1

the date line. So, it would be possible to celebrate your birthday on two consecutive days if you crossed the line in a ship headed from west to east. Or you could miss it altogether if you crossed the line from east to west at midnight.

The continental United States is divided into four time zones. From west to east these are Pacific, mountain, central, and eastern time. Notice that the boundaries of the zones are somewhat irregular. State boundary lines are often used so that different

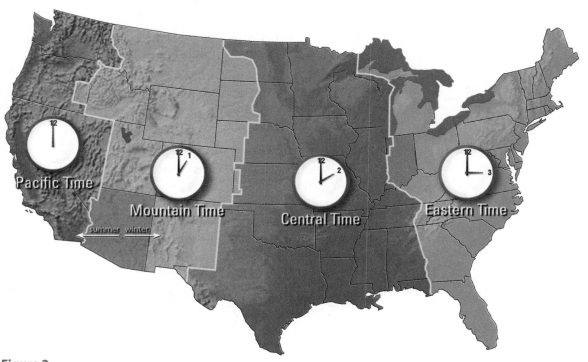

Figure 2

parts of a state are not in different time zones. However, a number of states are divided into two different time zones.

Since the earth rotates from west to east, people in the eastern time zone are the first to experience a given time. Those in the central time zone experience it an hour later. Those in the mountain time zone experience it two hours later. And those in the Pacific time zone experience it three hours later.

1. What time is it in New York City (eastern time) when it is 6:00 AM in Los Angeles (Pacific time)?

_____

2. What time is it in Chicago (central time) when it is 12:00 midnight in New York City (eastern time)?

_____

3. Is it possible for it to be Friday on the East Coast while it is Thursday on the West Coast?

_____

4. When it is 1:00 PM in New York City (eastern time), what time is it in Denver (mountain time)?

_____

5. When it is 7:00 PM in San Francisco (Pacific time), what time is it in New Orleans (central time)?

_____

Recalling that the earth rotates from west to east, you can understand why England is five hours ahead of eastern time and eight hours ahead of Pacific time. The time in England has a special significance. Called *Greenwich Mean Time* (GMT), it is standard time everywhere in the world. GMT is a 24-hour system, so it does not use am and pm. The morning hours run from 0 to 12. The afternoon and evening hours run from 12 to 24. Four digits are always used: the first two are the hour and the last two are the minutes past the hour. Thus, 10:30 AM is written 1030 GMT. For the morning hours before 10:00 AM, a zero is the first digit. So, 8:30 AM is 0830 GMT.

6. What is the eastern time when the time in England is 1500 GMT?

_____

7. What is the GMT when it is 2:00 AM in Boston (eastern time)?

_____

8. What time is it in Sacramento (Pacific time) when the time in England is 2230 GMT?

_____

4 GEOLOGY—THE EARTH SPEAKS

4A Catching Some Rays

name_____

section_____ date_____

What causes the seasons? And why are some parts of the earth hotter or colder than others? As your textbook explains, the earth's tilt is a major factor. Sunlight strikes some parts of the earth directly, while other parts get sunlight at an angle. Different exposure to sunlight causes different amounts of heating. That's the reason the seasons change and also why some parts of the world are hot while others are cold. How does the sunlight's angle determine its heating effect?

Sometimes scientists create *physical models* to explore a natural process or system. A physical model is often a miniature version of the system being explored. We're going to create a heating model of the sun and earth. Then we'll be able to explore how the sun heats the earth.

Procedure

- To make the solar heating device, cut out the solar heating device template. Glue the template onto the cardboard and trim away the excess. Fold the strips at the appropriate places, but don't tape them together yet.

- With the shorter strip flat on a table, place a good-sized drop of wax from a burning candle at points *A*, *B*, and *C*. Each drop should be about the same size. Allow five minutes for the wax to harden before continuing.

- Tape the ends of the strips together, and then tape the apparatus to a vertical surface such as a chalkboard or other non-flammable surface. *Do not use a whiteboard as it may discolor from the heat.*

- Place a sheet of newspaper directly below the apparatus to catch dripping wax.

- Set up the heat lamp to shine on the solar heating device as shown in Figure 2. Do *not* turn on the lamp yet. The lamp should be far enough away to keep the rays approximately parallel and close enough that the wax will melt in the time allowed. This will depend on the wattage of the lamp. When the wax melts it will begin to run.

- Predict the order in which you expect the drops to melt. Record your prediction in the table at the top of the next page.

- Turn on the lamp and start the stopwatch. Observe the wax closely. Note the time when the wax forms a drop that begins to run. Record the order in which the drops melt as well as the time (in seconds) that it took.

Goals

After completing this lab, you will be able to

✓ create a sun-earth heating model.

✓ use the model to see how perpendicular and slanted solar rays heat the earth differently.

Equipment

solar heating device template (available on the Teacher's Toolkit CD and on the *EARTH SCIENCE* 4th Edition Resources webpage)

scissors

thin cardboard

glue stick

candle

tape

newspaper

heat lamp or halogen worklight

stopwatch

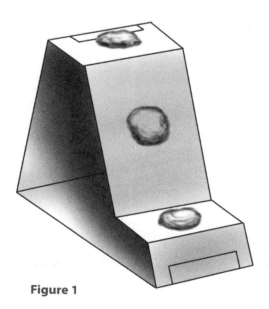

Figure 1

Figure 2 A sun-earth heating model

Predicted Melt Order	Actual Melt Order	Melt Time (s)

Now, let's look at heating in a little more detail. How hot each section gets depends on two factors. The first factor is the amount of heat energy coming from the lamp and falling on the model. Energy is measured in units called *joules* (J). We can assume that the energy from the lamp is consistent across the model. The second factor is the surface area of each section.

- Calculate the area of each section and record it in the table below.

We already know that the amount of heat energy coming from the lamp is uniform. However, the areas are not identical, so the heating will not be the same in each area.

1. Will a larger area be hotter or cooler than a smaller area? Why?

_____

_____

_____

We calculate the amount of energy absorbed by each section with the following formula:

$$\text{energy density} = \frac{\text{energy (J)}}{\text{area (cm}^2)}.$$

- Assume that 800 J of energy is reaching each section. Calculate the energy density for each section. Record it in the table.

Section of Model	Area (cm²)	Energy Density (J/cm²)
A		
B		
C		

2. Why did the wax melt earlier at some points than at others?

_____

_____

_____

3. Why did it take longer to melt the wax at point *B*, even though it was closer to the heat lamp, than the wax at point *C*?

_____

_____

_____

4. What could have caused the wax at point *A* to melt before the wax at point *C*?

_____

_____

_____

5. How does this model demonstrate the reason that the Equator is warmer than the poles?

_____

_____

6. How does this model demonstrate the reason that we have seasons?

_____

_____

_____

4B Listening to the Earth

name_____

section_____   date_____

How do we know what the inside of the earth looks like? The deepest hole is less than ten miles deep. As your textbook explains, earth scientists model the inside of the earth by *listening* to it. But what are they listening to?

Scientists listen to *seismic waves* moving through the earth. When the waves speed up or slow down, they bend, bounce, and spread out. Scientists know the speed of seismic waves in different materials. By timing the waves and monitoring their behavior, they can model the earth's interior.

Seismic waves are actually a special kind of sound wave. Normally we think of sounds as moving through air. But sound can move through solids and liquids as well. What determines how fast sound travels through solid objects?

1. List the properties of solid materials that you think might change the speed of sound in objects made of these materials.

_____

_____

Goals
After completing this lab, you will be able to
✓ identify factors that influence the speed of sound through solids.
✓ create a model to learn how a material's physical properties determine the speed of sound through it.
✓ discuss how the speed of sound in solids helps earth scientists look inside the earth.

Equipment
graph paper (included)

Sound waves cause solid materials to bend, stretch, and compress. So it makes sense that a material's *stiffness* might have something to do with how fast sound moves through it. We also know that dense materials have a lot of mass in a small space. It's harder for a wave to move a large mass than a small one. So it makes sense that density might also be part of the picture. Let's explore density and stiffness to see if they have anything to do with the speed of sound.

Figure 1 How fast do sound waves travel through copper?

Procedure
The table below lists eight common metals. Included is the typical speed of sound in that metal. The table also includes the metal's density and stiffness. The larger the stiffness number is, the stiffer the material.

Material	Speed of Sound (m/s)	Density (g/cm³)	Stiffness (GPa)
Lead (Pb)	700	11.3	6
Gold (Au)	1200	19.3	27
Silver (Ag)	1700	10.5	30
Copper (Cu)	2300	9.0	48
Zinc (Zn)	2500	7.1	43
Nickel (Ni)	3000	8.9	76
Aluminum (Al)	3100	2.7	26
Iron (Fe)	3200	7.9	82

- Using the first graphing area on page 44, create a graph that models density compared to the speed of sound. The *x*-axis is the speed of sound. The *y*-axis is the material's density. Label each point with the material's chemical symbol.
- Attempt to draw a smooth curve that moves only upward or downward between the points.

2. Do you see an obvious relationship between density and the speed of sound in a material? How do you know?

_____

_____

_____

- Using the second graphing area, create a graph that models stiffness compared to the speed of sound. The *x*-axis is the speed of sound. The *y*-axis is the material's stiffness. Label each point with the material's chemical symbol.
- Attempt to draw a smooth curve that moves only upward or downward between the points.

3. Do you see an obvious relationship between stiffness and the speed of sound in a material? How do you know?

_____

_____

_____

We don't seem to be getting anywhere! Perhaps the speed of sound has something to do with *both* density and stiffness. Let's try out this idea by combining the two properties.

- Calculate the ratio of stiffness to density by dividing stiffness by density. Round your answer to one decimal place and record it in the table below.

Material	Ratio of Stiffness and Density
Lead (Pb)	
Gold (Au)	
Silver (Ag)	
Copper (Cu)	
Zinc (Zn)	
Nickel (Ni)	
Aluminum (Al)	
Iron (Fe)	

- Using the graphing area (on page 45), create a graph that models the stiffness/density ratio compared to the speed of sound. The x-axis is the speed of sound. The y-axis is the ratio. Label each point with the material's chemical symbol.

- Attempt to draw a smooth curve that moves only upward or downward between the points.

4. Do you see an obvious relationship between the ratio and the speed of sound in a material? How do you know?

_____

_____

_____

5. What appears to control the speed of sound in solid materials?

_____

6. Think back to what you learned in Labs 2A and 2B. Do you think pressure and temperature could affect the speed of sound? If so, explain how.

_____

_____

_____

7. In what way is your model simpler than the interior of the earth (especially the crust and the mantle)?

_____

_____

_____

8. In what way does your model approximate the earth's core very well?

_____

_____

_____

Density vs. Speed of Sound

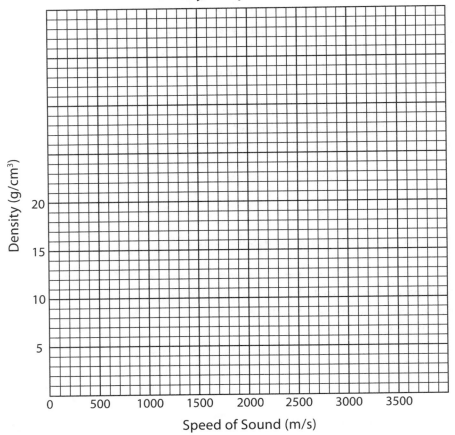

Stiffness vs. Speed of Sound

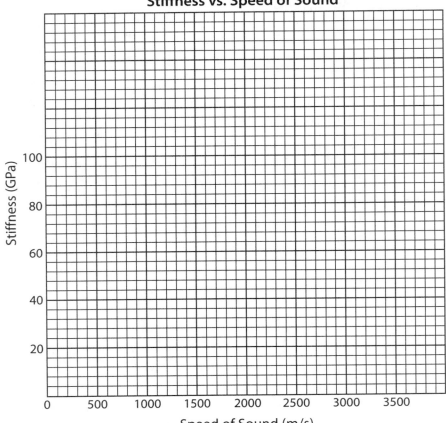

name_____

Ratio of Stiffness & Density vs. Speed of Sound

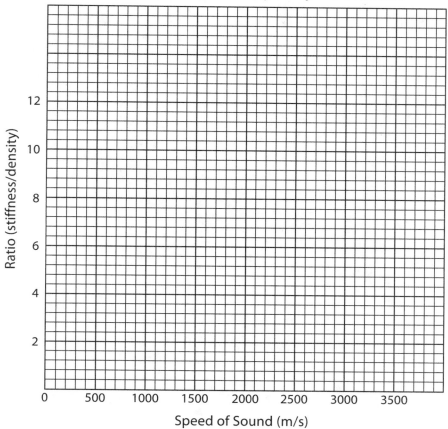

5 THE CHANGING EARTH

5A Where Do Those Dates Come From?

How old is the earth? This question lies at the heart of both Christian and secular worldviews. Young-earth creationists say that the earth is less than 10,000 years old. Some give more precise ages such as 6000 or 7000 years. In 1650, Archbishop James Ussher said that God created the earth in 4004 BC. Where do these dates come from? Are they just guesses, or is there some kind of calculation behind them?

When a young-earth creationist gives a specific age, such as 7000 years, he usually bases it on Bible *chronology*. In other words, he uses the birth, death, and age records in the Bible to calculate a list of times. This list helps him calculate the age of the earth. Let's try our hand at Bible chronology.

Procedure

- We begin our chronology with Adam since he was the first human and was created just five days after the earth itself. But what date do we use for Adam's creation? We don't know "how many years BC" Adam was born!

1. What year should we use for Adam's creation? (*Hint*: Review the margin box on page 99 in your textbook.)

   _____

- Now we need to figure out when Adam's son Seth was born. For this information, we turn to Genesis 5:3.

2. How old was Adam when Seth was born? What year AM was Seth born?

   _____

   _____

- Use Genesis 5 to complete the chart on the top of the next page. To calculate the date of the Flood, you'll have to look at Genesis 7:11.

name_____

section_____   date_____

Figure 1 The Bible is the key to dating the earth.

Event	Year (AM)
Adam created	0
Seth born	130
Enos born	
Cainan born	
Mahalaleel born	
Jared born	
Enoch born	
Methuselah born	
Lamech born	
Noah born	
Flood begins	

- To go further forward in time, we need to look at other Bible passages. Genesis 11 contains another chronology that continues up to the birth of Abraham. Other chapters in Genesis give us additional names and ages. The table below shows these dates.

Event	Year (AM)
Arphaxad born	1658
Cainan born	1793
Salah born	1923
Eber born	2053
Peleg born	2187
Reu born	2317
Serug born	2449
Nahor born	2579
Terah born	2758
Abraham born	2888
Isaac born	2988
Jacob born	3048

Texts and Translations

The dates presented in this table are based on the Greek translation of the Old Testament. This translation is known as the Septuagint (also called the LXX). It was produced in the Egyptian city of Alexandria between the third and second centuries BC. On the other hand, most English Bible translations are based on the Masoretic Text (MT), a group of Hebrew manuscripts dating from the ninth century AD.

You may wonder why we're using the Septuagint text instead of the one our Bibles are based on. The reason is that Arphaxad's son Cainan is missing from the MT but present in the LXX. How do we know he really belongs there at all? We know he belongs because his name appears in Jesus's genealogy, recorded in Luke 3:36. So, in this particular case, the New Testament authenticates the Septuagint version of the genealogy. That's why we're using it here.

- We now come to an important biblical event: Jacob's family moving to Egypt (Gen. 46:5–6). Can we know what year this event happened? Read Genesis 47:7–9.

3. What year did Jacob's family move to Egypt?

_____

- Israel left Egypt many years later (the Exodus). Do we know the year of the Exodus? Read Exodus 12:40–41.

4. What year did the Exodus happen?

name_____

_____

    Years AM are interesting, but they don't relate to the calendar dating system used by modern historians. It would be nice to know what these years are "BC." Is there any way to handle this problem?

    We can solve the problem if we can connect one of these dates to an event whose historical date BC we know. And the Bible gives us just such an event: the building of Solomon's Temple. Historians are fairly confident that the construction of Solomon's Temple started in 966 BC. But how can we connect this date to the dates we've just calculated?

- The Bible tells us that Solomon started building the Temple 480 years after the Exodus (1 Kings 6:1).

5. What year AM did Solomon start building the Temple?

_____

- So we know that the AM date you just calculated is the same as 966 BC.

6. What year BC did God create the earth?

_____

7. How old is the earth right now?

_____

8. Should we say that the earth is *exactly* this number of years old? Why or why not?

_____

_____

_____

_____

_____

5B What's Your Lifespan?

How long will you live? Probably everyone would love to know the answer to that question! Statistics can give you an idea of how long you can expect to live. If you were born in the United States in 2000, statistics say that you can expect to reach your mid to late 70s. Of course, God decides how long He keeps us on the earth.

The Flood changed the earth in many ways. It helped to form mountains, canyons, and caves. It probably changed the climate. And it affected human life in ways that must have been very startling to those born after the Flood. Before the Flood, people frequently lived for over 900 years. After the Flood, human lifespan started dropping rapidly. Think how you would feel if you knew that your lifespan would be much less than that of your grandparents or even your parents!

The Bible gives us some very useful data about human lifespan after the Flood. Genesis 11:10–32 lists the ages of nine people. Other verses in Genesis give us additional names and ages. We can use this data to explore how human lifespan changed.

Procedure

- Turn to the Appendix in the back of this book. It contains several excerpts of Genesis taken from the Septuagint (LXX) translation of the Old Testament. As you learned in Lab 5A, the Septuagint's post-Flood genealogies are probably the most accurate available to us.

- Look at Genesis 11:12–13 in the LXX text. Notice that it does not give us Arphaxad's age when he died. Instead, it tells us how many years he lived after his son Cainan was born.

1. How do you think we can calculate Arphaxad's total age?

_____

_____

_____

The table on the next page lists in the first column each person's name and the place in the Bible where his name appears. The next column lists how many years after the Flood (AF) he was born. The final column, the person's lifespan, is blank.

- Complete the table by using the LXX text to find each person's lifespan. You will have to calculate some ages like you did with Arphaxad. The Bible gives some ages directly.

name_____

section_____   date_____

Goals

After completing this lab, you will be able to
- ✓ use Bible genealogies to study life after the Flood.
- ✓ graph data to identify trends in human lifespan.
- ✓ discuss how human lifespan changed after the Flood.

Equipment

graph paper (provided)

Figure 1 Your family history helps you estimate your lifespan.

Name & Reference	Year Born (AF)	Lifespan (years)
Arphaxad (Gen. 11:12–13)	2	
Cainan (Gen. 11:13)	137	
Salah (Gen. 11:14–15)	267	
Eber (Gen. 11:16–17)	397	
Peleg (Gen. 11:18–19)	531	
Reu (Gen. 11:20–21)	661	
Serug (Gen. 11:22–23)	793	
Nahor (Gen. 11:24–25)	923	
Terah (Gen. 11:32)	1102	
Abraham (Gen. 25:7)	1232	
Isaac (Gen. 35:28)	1332	
Jacob (Gen. 47:28)	1392	
Joseph (Gen. 50:26)	1483	

- Using the graphing area on the next page, create a graph that models how human lifespan changed after the Flood. The *x*-axis is the number of years after the Flood (AF) the person was born. The *y*-axis is the person's lifespan.

- Draw a smooth curve between the points.

2. What happened to human lifespan after the Flood?

_____

3. Did it change by a lot or just a little?

_____

4. Did each person live a shorter life than his father? Explain.

_____

_____

_____

5. If you were born 200 years after the Flood, about how long could you expect to live?

_____

6. How much shorter was Abraham's lifespan than his grandfather Nahor's?

_____

7. Is this condition still true today? Explain.

name_____

_____

_____

_____

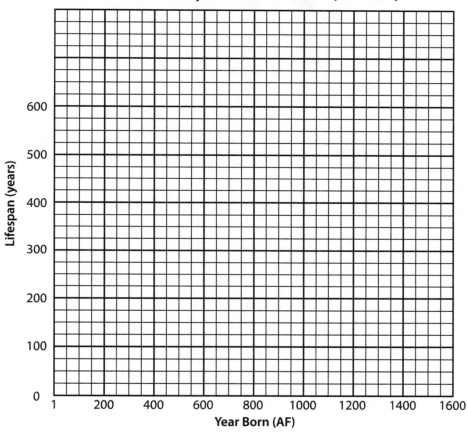

Human Lifespan After the Flood (LXX text)

5C Going with the Flow

name_____

section_____   date_____

Have you ever noticed that it's warmer near the ceiling than the floor? You probably also know that warm air rises. Why is this so? The answer is *density*. Labs 2A and 2B explored density, so you should remember that density is the ratio of a substance's mass to its volume. Solids, liquids, and gases all have density.

As you saw in Lab 2B, density can change with temperature. When you cooled the liquids, their densities changed. If we heat a substance, it expands, so its density becomes lower. That's why warm air rises. It's less dense than cold air; so as gravity pulls the cold air down, the cold air pushes the warm air up.

The earth's mantle is like a very thick liquid since it's made of molten rock. Rock lower down in the mantle is hotter than rock near the crust. Cooler rock near the top is denser, so it tends to sink. Hot rock from below gets pushed up in plumes toward the upper mantle because it's less dense. If we could watch the mantle, we would see an endless flow of hot rock upward and cooler rock downward. This motion is called *convection*.

We can't visit the mantle, but we can make a model of it in the laboratory.

Goals

After completing this lab, you will be able to
✓ describe how density changes with heat.
✓ model density currents in the mantle.

Equipment

beaker, 50 mL
beaker, 200 mL
eyedropper or pipette
glycerin
food coloring

Procedure

- Fill the 200 mL beaker with 125 mL of cold glycerin.

- Fill the 50 mL beaker with 25 mL of room-temperature glycerin. Add a drop of food coloring to the glycerin and stir well. The food coloring will make the glycerin easy to see.

1. Which is denser, warm or cold glycerin?

   _____

2. If you add the room-temperature glycerin to the bottom of the container of cold glycerin, what do you expect to happen?

   _____

   _____

   _____

- Fill the pipette with room-temperature glycerin. Slowly insert the pipette into the beaker of cold glycerin until it is near the bottom. Try to avoid stirring up the liquid.

- Release the glycerin into the bottom of the beaker. Slowly remove the pipette so you don't stir up the liquid.

- Watch the behavior of the room-temperature glycerin. Draw a series of sketches showing its behavior over a 15-minute period.

- You may wish to create several glycerin plumes in different locations and observe their behavior.

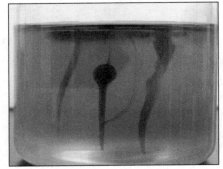

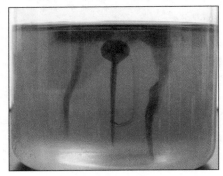

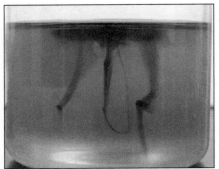

Figure 1 A model of the mantle

3. Did the glycerin behave as expected? Explain.

_____

_____

_____

4. Discuss how your glycerin model approximates the behavior of magma within the mantle.

_____

_____

_____

6 EARTHQUAKES

6A Quake Watcher

name _____

section _____   date _____

As we've already learned, scientists spend much of their time working with data. Sometimes they use their senses to gather it. But what do you do when you can't detect what you want to measure? And what if you want to measure something 24/7? Very few people like to stay awake continuously!

In these situations, scientists rely on *instruments* to collect data. Instruments can be much more sensitive and specialized than our senses. And instruments never sleep, so they can collect vast amounts of data automatically.

Instruments are ideal for monitoring earthquakes. Many quakes are too small for the senses to detect. *Seismographs* are sensitive scientific instruments designed to measure and record the shaking of the earth during earthquakes. A seismoscope is similar to a seismograph, but it only indicates *when* an earthquake occurs. It does not record and store the quake's data for later retrieval. In this lab, you will make a simple seismoscope.

Procedure

- Set up the ring stand and clamp the base to one table with the C-clamp. Secure the right-angle support clamp near the top of the ring stand rod. Then, secure the dowel rod in the clamp. The dowel rod should extend over the second desktop.
- Strip 3 cm of insulation from each end of all three wires.
- Tie the fishing sinker about 2 cm above the stripped end of one wire. The bare wire should extend below the sinker. We call the sinker the *inertial mass* of the instrument.
- Tie the length of wire with the sinker to the dowel so that the bare wire below the sinker hangs 2–3 mm above the second desktop. Adjust the height with the right-angle clamp.
- Connect one end of the second wire to one of the terminals on the light socket.
- Form the stripped portion of one end of the third wire into a small circular loop 5–7 mm in diameter. Bend the loop so that it's perpendicular to the long part of the wire. Carefully thread the hanging wire through the loop. Then, secure the loop in place with a piece of clay. When all pieces are assembled and stationary, the bare end of the hanging wire should be inside the center of the loop but not actually touching it.
- Connect the free end of the third wire to the other terminal on the light socket.
- Connect the free ends of the first and second wires to the battery terminals.

Goals
After completing this lab, you will be able to
✓ explain why instruments are important in science.
✓ build and demonstrate a simple seismoscope.
✓ discuss how a seismoscope works.

Equipment
desks or tables, same height (2)
ring stand
C-clamp
right-angle support clamp
dowel rod, 1/4 in.
6 V lantern battery
6 V light bulb and socket
insulated wire, #24–#26, 1 m (3)
fishing sinker (1–6 oz, heavier is better)
modeling clay

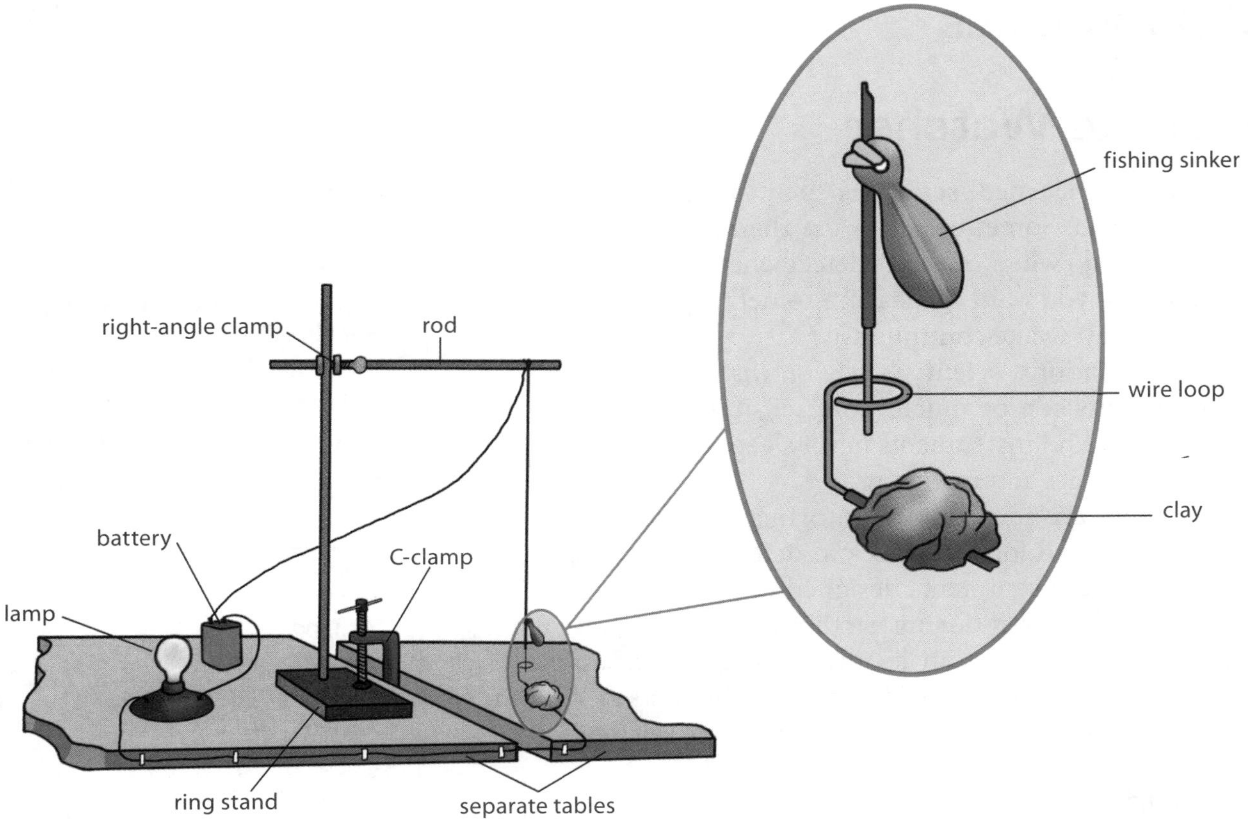

right-angle clamp   rod

fishing sinker

wire loop

clay

battery

lamp

C-clamp

ring stand   separate tables

Figure 1

1. Gently bump the second table. What happens?

_____

_____

2. Shake the table harder. What happens?

_____

_____

3. Bump the table hard enough to move the table on the floor. What happens?

_____

_____

4. How does the flashing change with the strength of the bump?

_____

_____

5. What does bumping the table represent?

_____

_____

6. Which part of the seismoscope is moving during the "earth-quake," the loop or the inertial mass?

name _____

_____

7. How could this seismoscope be made more sensitive?

_____

_____

_____

8. How could the movement of the table be permanently recorded?

_____

_____

9. What would this instrument be called if it were modified so that it could record earthquake data for later use?

_____

6B Where Did It Start?

We all know that too much stress is bad for you. It's not good in the earth's crust either! When stress builds up within the crust, bad things can happen. Normally, tectonic plates and faults glide past each other. But sometimes their boundaries catch, and stress starts building up. Eventually, the stress becomes too great and there is a sudden release of energy. When that happens, we experience an earthquake.

As your textbook explains, earthquakes are waves of energy moving through the earth. These *seismic waves* are similar to sound waves but are much more powerful. Two different kinds of waves, called P and S waves, travel through the earth at different speeds. Scientists can use the arrival time difference between these waves to answer an important question: Where did the earthquake start?

Earthquakes begin at a point deep within the earth called the *focus*. The focus is the place where the stress got too great. Seismic waves spread out from the focus in all directions. The geographic location directly above the focus is called the *epicenter*. Let's use some seismic wave data to pinpoint the epicenter of an earthquake.

name_____

section_____ date_____

Goals

After completing this lab, you will be able to

✓ establish the location of an earthquake's epicenter using data from three seismic stations.

✓ compare the relative energies of different quakes from their magnitude ratings.

Equipment

calculator
drawing compass
map or atlas of the United States

Procedure

The table below shows the data collected by three seismic monitoring stations for a single earthquake. Each record gives the arrival time of the earthquake's P and S waves as well as the quake's relative magnitude (M_L) reading.

Date	Station	ID	LAT	LONG	Elev (m)	P Wave hh:mm:ss (UTC)	S Wave hh:mm:ss (UTC)	M_L	Sensor
28JUL05	Elko, NV	ELK	40.7448	−115.2388	2210.0	18:11:01.7	18:11:59.2	7.8	BB
28JUL05	Eugene, OR	EUO	44.0294	−123.0689	160.0	18:11:10.5	18:12:15.9	7.8	BB
28JUL05	Sta Barbara, CA	SBC	34.4408	−119.7149	61.0	18:11:01.1	18:11:51.8	7.8	BB

To locate the epicenter, we need to know how far away we are from it. The first step is determining the time difference between the arrival of the P and S waves.

- Calculate the time difference between the P and S waves for each station ($t_S - t_P$). Record the times in the table on the next page.

- Next, calculate the distance from each station to the epicenter by using the following formula. Round your answers to the nearest kilometer and record them in the table.

$$d = 9.33 \, (t_S - t_P)$$

Figure 1 Seismic monitoring stations like this one help scientists locate and measure earthquakes.

Station	$t_S - t_P$ (s)	Distance (d) from epicenter (km)
Elko, NV		
Eugene, OR		
Santa Barbara, CA		

- On the map below, use the compass to draw a circle around the Elko, Nevada, station with a radius equal to the distance from the station to the epicenter. Use the map scale to adjust the compass legs to the correct radius.

Figure 2

1. What does the circle represent?

_____

_____

Obviously, the circle narrows down the possible locations of the epicenter. But it doesn't let us pinpoint it with precision. Let's add another circle.

- Draw a circle around the Eugene, Oregon, station. Be sure to readjust the compass to the correct radius before drawing the circle.

2. Can we pinpoint the epicenter now? Why or why not?

_____

_____

- Draw a circle around the Santa Barbara, California, station. Be sure to readjust the compass to the correct radius before drawing the circle.

3. Can we pinpoint the epicenter now? Why or why not?

_____

_____

- Using a map, atlas, or GIS tool, locate the largest major city near the epicenter. Label the epicenter with the city's name.

4. Where is the epicenter located?

_____

Knowing an earthquake's strength is also important. Small quakes cause minimal damage, while large ones can have enormous costs in life and property. You may wish to review Subsection 6.10 in your textbook before answering the following questions.

5. Which quake had more energy, the one explored in this lab or one rated magnitude 6.8?

_____

6. How *much* more energy did the stronger quake have?

_____

7. Examine Table 6-1 in your textbook. Based on the magnitude of this lab's earthquake, what kind of damage would you expect?

_____

_____

6C All Quiet?

Most people think of earthquakes as rare events. When they happen, they're major news, like the Haiti earthquake of January 12, 2010, or the Japanese earthquake/tsunami of March 11, 2011. But is this idea correct? Is the earth ever truly quiet?

Actually, it isn't! You'd be surprised how seismically noisy the earth is. While we cannot predict *when* large earthquakes will occur, we do know *where* they are likely to happen. Your textbook discusses the causes of earthquakes. Tectonic plate motion causes stress to build up in underground rock layers. If the layers suddenly crack or slip, an earthquake happens.

1. Where does this stress tend to build up?

   _____

   _____

2. How would you find the places on Earth where earthquakes are most likely to occur?

   _____

   _____

   _____

Let's check your ideas with Google Earth™, a GIS tool that we can customize for earthquake study. By itself, the program doesn't display any information about tectonic plates. But Google Earth™ has an important feature. You can add extra thematic information with external files created by other people. These are called KML or KMZ files. There are thousands of them available on the Internet. With the right file, Google Earth™ can help you study almost any earth science topic!

Procedure

- Start Google Earth.™ Your teacher will give you a KMZ file that adds a tectonic plate thematic layer. Load the file by selecting **File | Open** and browsing to the file. Select the file and click **Open**.

- Find the **Temporary Places** checkbox on the left side of the screen and check it. Google Earth™ shows the tectonic plate boundaries as colored lines.

3. Which color represents convergent plate boundaries?

   _____

name _____

section _____   date _____

Goals

After completing this lab, you will be able to

✓ predict probable locations for earthquakes.

✓ view tectonic plate boundaries using a GIS system.

✓ monitor current earthquake activity using a GIS system.

Equipment

computer with Google Earth™

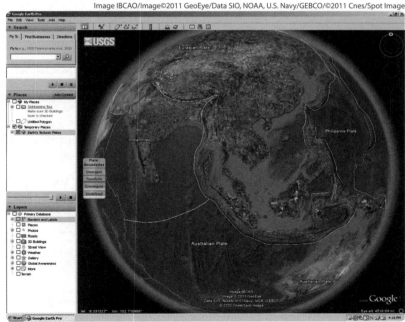

Image IBCAO/Image©2011 GeoEye/Data SIO, NOAA, U.S. Navy/GEBCO/©2011 Cnes/Spot Image

Figure 1

Figure 2 Thingvellir National Park in Iceland is part of the Mid-Atlantic Ridge, the border between two tectonic plates.

- Spend a few minutes exploring the globe to see where all the plates are located. If you zoom in so your **Eye alt** is 5000 mi (8047 km) or less, the plate names will be visible.

4. How many plates make up North America? Name it/them.

_____

_____

_____

- **Fly to** the island country of Iceland, located in the North Atlantic.

5. From a tectonic point of view, what is unusual about Iceland?

_____

_____

_____

- The city of San Francisco, California, has a long history of earthquakes. **Fly to** San Francisco.

6. What do you notice about this city in relation to the tectonic plates? Do you think this relationship has anything to do with its earthquake history?

_____

_____

_____

7. What kind of plate boundary exists at this point?

_____

8. Based upon what you've learned in your textbook, describe the plate motion at this boundary.

_____

_____

- The island country of Japan is also known for its powerful earthquakes. **Fly to** Japan and examine its relationship to the tectonic plates.

9. How many plates make up the area surrounding Japan? Name it/them.

_____

_____

_____

10. What kind of boundary exists between these plates?

name _____

_____

11. Based upon what you've learned, what are the most likely places to find earthquakes?

_____

_____

- Let's test your hypothesis. Spend a few minutes examining the plate boundaries. Pick three locations that you think should be *likely* candidates for earthquakes. Pick three locations that you think should be *unlikely* candidates for earthquakes. Avoid familiar locations so you won't be biased by prior knowledge. List your choices in the table below:

Likely	Confirm?	Unlikely	Confirm?

- Your teacher will direct you to a location on the USGS (U.S. Geological Survey) website. This website provides up-to-the-minute reports on earthquake activity all over the world. When you link this information to Google Earth,™ you can see earthquakes as they're happening!

- Once you've found the correct website, your teacher will direct you to select a particular link to open the USGS real-time earthquake KML file. When you select the link, the file will open in Google Earth.™

Image IBCAO/Image©2011 GeoEye/Data SIO, NOAA, U.S. Navy/GEBCO/©2011 Cnes/Spot Image

- The USGS file displays its own set of tectonic plate boundaries. These use a different color scheme, however, so you must turn them off. Locate the **USGS Real-time earthquakes** list under the **Temporary Places** box and uncheck **Tectonic Plate Boundaries**.

- The new KML file displays all world earthquake activity for the past seven days. Circles represent earthquakes. Look at the legend that explains what the circles mean.

Figure 3

12. What two pieces of information do the circles represent? Explain.

_____

_____

- For more information, place the mouse pointer on a circle. It will expand and display the earthquake's date, magnitude, and location.
- Go to the three locations where you predicted likely earthquake activity. If the data from Google Earth™ confirms your prediction, put a *Y* in the table's "Confirm?" column. If your prediction was wrong, put an *N* in the column.
- Go to the three locations where you predicted that earthquake activity is unlikely. If the data from Google Earth™ confirms your prediction, put a *Y* in the table's "Confirm?" column. If your prediction was wrong, put an *N* in the column.

13. Overall, was your hypothesis correct? Explain.

_____

_____

14. Quickly survey the major divergent plate boundaries all over the globe. Are they likely places for earthquakes? Why or why not?

_____

_____

15. Scan the globe again. Which areas appear to be unusually active seismically?

_____

_____

_____

16. Is the earth as quiet as most people assume? Explain.

_____

_____

17. Knowing all of this, what do you think should be the future focus of seismology in order to best use the world's land resources and to help people?

_____

_____

_____

7 MOUNTAINS AND HILLS

7A How High?

name _____

section _____   date _____

Imagine yourself an explorer in the early 1800s. You've been hiking along for weeks, when suddenly you come to an unusually tall mountain. Like any good explorer, you've been making a map of the places you've visited. Naturally, you want to include the mountain on your map.

Surveying its base is easy enough, but how do you measure its height? Remember, this is the early 1800s. GPS and satellite imaging are almost two centuries in the future. Portable altimeters (altitude-measuring instruments) won't be available for another 75 years. You can't climb to the top and unroll a tape measure! What do you do?

As you learned in Lab 3B, scientists sometimes use *indirect measurement* when it isn't possible to measure something directly. An indirect measurement takes something that you *can* measure and turns it into a measurement of something that you *can't* measure. Surveyors often use indirect measurement techniques too. Many of the things they examine can't be measured directly. Let's see how this process works.

> **Goals**
>
> After completing this lab, you will be able to
> ✓ explain the reason surveyors often use indirect measurement techniques.
> ✓ measure a tall object indirectly.
> ✓ compare the measured and actual heights.

> **Equipment**
>
> protractor
> centimeter ruler
> string or thread, 40 cm
> weight (large nut or fishing sinker)
> large-diameter drinking straw
> tape measure (15 m or longer)

Procedure

- Look at the two triangles shown below. Using the ruler, measure each of the sides to the nearest 0.1 cm (1 mm). Using the protractor, measure angle X to the nearest 1°. Record the measurements in the blanks below the triangles.

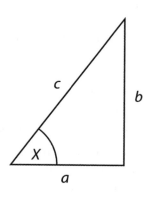

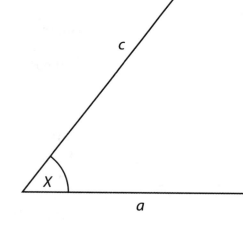

a _____

b _____

c _____

X _____

a _____

b _____

c _____

X _____

1. What do you notice about angle *X* of each triangle?

_____

2. What do you notice about the sides?

_____

_____

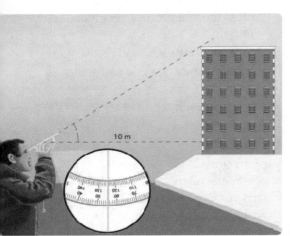

Figure 1 Using a clinometer to measure a building's height

We call triangles like these *similar triangles*. They are identical except for size. All of their angles match, and their sides have the same proportions, even though they are different lengths. We're going to use the principle of similar triangles to measure tall objects.

- If you completed Lab 3A, you've already built a *clinometer*, an angle-measuring instrument. If not, go back to Lab 3A and follow the instructions to build the clinometer.

- Find a tall object such as a building, telephone pole, or tree.

- Using the tape measure, measure 10 m from the object's base. Be cautious about traffic, and avoid getting in other people's way.

- Stand at the 10 m location and look through the straw. Tilt the protractor until you see the top of the object.

- Have a partner look at the string, which should be hanging straight down. Read the number that the string passes through. If the protractor has two sets of numbers, use the number that is between 0 and 90. Record the number below.

_____

- Subtract this number from 90.° The answer is the angle formed between the top of the object, your eyes, and the line along the ground. Record the result below.

_____

- Now we need to draw a triangle like the one formed by the building, your eyes, and the ground. The triangle on your paper will be smaller, but it will have the same proportions.

- On a sheet of paper, draw a horizontal line 10 cm long. This will represent the 10 m distance between the base of the object and the place where you stood.

3. What is the scale of your paper triangle compared to the object? (*Hint*: How much smaller is the line on the paper than the distance to the object?)

_____

- Using the protractor, draw a line from one end of the base line, tilted to the same angle that you calculated above.

- Finally, draw a vertical line from the other end of the base line until it intersects the angled line. This line represents the height of the object.

- Using the ruler, measure the vertical line to the nearest 0.1 cm (1 mm). This value is the scaled height of the object. Record it below.

_____

4. What must you do to turn the scaled height into the actual height?

_____

_____

5. What is the actual height of the object?

_____

- There is a problem with your measurement. Your triangles are drawn with their base lines on the ground. But the actual triangle has its base at the height of your eyes.

6. What must you add to your calculated height to fix the problem?

_____

_____

7. What is the corrected height of the object?

_____

8. The explorer mentioned at the beginning of the lab measures a mountain using the method we've just explored. He stands 2 km from the base of the mountain. Using his clinometer, he measures the angle between the base and the summit and finds it to be 20.° What is the mountain's height?

_____

name_____

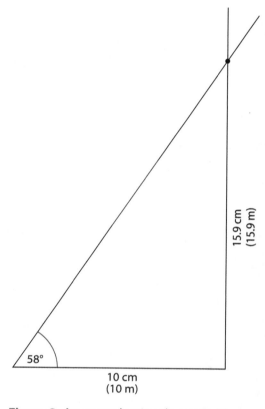

15.9 cm
(15.9 m)

58°

10 cm
(10 m)

Figure 2 An example triangle created from data

Optional Activity

If you know the actual height of the object you measured, you can check your measurement's accuracy. If you measured a building, you might be able to find its height from the building manager. Many well-known public buildings have their heights published on the Internet.

- Calculate the percent error between the actual height of the object and the indirectly measured height. Percent error was discussed in Lab 2B. Record the result below.

_____

1. Based upon the error standards mentioned in Lab 2B, how good was your indirect measurement?

_____

_____

7B Mapping a Modeled Mountain

name _____

section _____ date _____

Mountains are three-dimensional objects, but paper is flat. When scientists create maps of mountains, they need to come up with a way to make a 3D object into a 2D one. One way is to create two maps of the mountain. One, called a *relief map*, is a picture of the mountain from above. The other, a *profile map*, is a view from the side.

In this lab, we're going to build a small physical model of a mountain and then take a series of measurements from it. We'll use these to create a relief map of the mountain. Once we complete the relief map, we'll use it to create a profile map.

Procedure

- Fashion a mountain approximately 10–15 cm high out of modeling clay. The model should be a few centimeters shorter than the depth of the dishpan. It should fit within the blank drawing area on page 76. Make one side of the mountain noticeably steeper than the other. Try to give it interesting features.

- Place the mountain model in the dishpan. Tape the ruler vertically to the inside wall of the dishpan.

A relief map indicates altitude and landforms by color, shading, or some other device. For more precise elevation information, relief maps are printed with *contour lines*. An elevation contour line connects all points on the map that are at the same elevation above a reference height—usually average sea level. Contour lines on the map are labeled with their elevation. Where lines are close together, only every fifth or tenth line may be labeled. The diagram below gives you an idea of how a contour relief map should look.

> ### Goals
> After completing this lab, you will be able to
> ✓ construct a physical model of a mountain.
> ✓ create a relief map of the model mountain.
> ✓ use the relief map to create a profile map.

> ### Equipment
> waterproof modeling clay
> deep dishpan or large pot with straight sides
> plastic centimeter ruler
> water pitcher or large beaker
> old ballpoint pen or pointed clay tool
> 3×5 index card

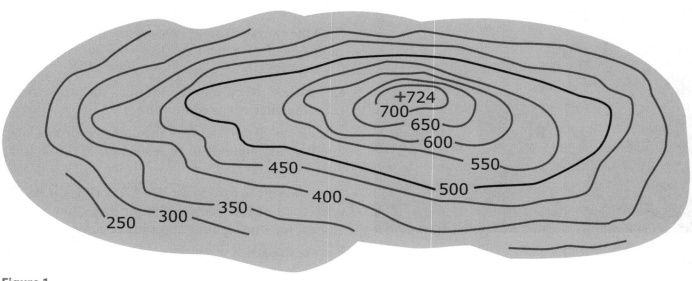

Figure 1

- Using the pitcher, slowly pour water into the dishpan to a depth of 1 cm.

- Using the ballpoint pen point or clay tool, scratch a line all the way around the mountain at the water line.

- Add another centimeter of water and scratch another contour line at the water line.

- Repeat the process, adding 1 cm of water and scratching a contour line until the entire mountain is submerged.

- Carefully pour the water out of the container and observe the mountain from above.

- Draw a relief map of the model as accurately as you can in the blank drawing area on page 76. Include centimeter values to show the level of each contour line.

1. What does close contour spacing tell you about the mountain?

_____

_____

2. How would the summit of the mountain be represented on your map?

_____

A relief map shows you the elevation levels of a mountain as observed from the top. A profile map shows what the mountain looks like from the side. If you already have a relief map, it's possible to use it to construct a profile map quite easily.

- Using the ruler, draw a horizontal line that passes through your relief map's mountain peak. This line is called the *profile reference line.*

- Take the index card and place the narrow edge on the 1 cm line of the blank profile map that is directly below your relief map. You are going to use the card to help you draw straight, parallel lines.

- Slide the card so its right long edge is all the way to the right side of the relief map. Keep the narrow edge on the 1 cm line.

- Slowly slide the card to the left until the profile reference line intersects a contour line.

- Draw a small vertical line through the profile map line that corresponds to the elevation of the contour line.

- Keep sliding the card to the left. Every time the profile reference line intersects a contour line, draw a small vertical line through the appropriate elevation line.

- Be sure to mark a vertical line for the summit's elevation as well.

Figure 2 Using the card to draw the profile map

- When you've finished, draw a smooth line through the places where the vertical lines intersect the elevation lines. You've just profiled your mountain!

3. If the contour lines on a relief map are far apart, how does that correspond to the appearance of the mountain's profile?

_____

_____

4. What does a profile map visually show you about contour lines that are close together?

_____

_____

5. Why would relief maps and profile diagrams be important for geologists and engineers?

_____

_____

_____

_____

elevation (cm)

15
14
13
12
11
10
9
8
7
6
5
4
3
2
1

7C Staying on Top of It

Reading maps is a crucial skill for any geologist who studies mountains and hills. A *topographic map* is a map that represents the three-dimensional shape of the earth's surface. Topographic maps display many features. These include *relief* (differences in height from one point to the next), *water features* (lakes, streams, swamps), and *man-made features* (roads, bridges, tunnels, railroad tracks).

A map's *scale* helps you determine distances between features. With nothing more than a ruler or a pair of dividers, you can measure distances easily. A typical scale is 1:24,000. With this scale, every distance in the real world is 24,000 times as large as the same distance measured on the map.

We're going to sharpen our map skills by studying a portion of northwestern Montana. The name *Montana* comes from the Spanish word meaning "mountainous." Quite fittingly, mountains are prominent on both the state flag and the state seal of Montana.

Procedure

- The United States-Canada border runs along the top of the map on page 79 from corner to corner. Using the dividers and the map scale, determine in kilometers how far south Chief Mountain is from the border. Record the distance below.

  _____

- Using the ruler and the map scale, determine the aerial distance in kilometers from the summit of Mt. Siyeh (south of Siyeh Glacier) to the summit of Chief Mountain. Record it below.

  _____

- Find and record the elevation of the following features listed in the table below.

Feature	Elevation (m)
Apikuni Mountain	
Mt. Wilbur	
Mt. Cleveland	
Mt. Cannon	
Yellow Mountain	
Mt. Grinnell	
Allen Mountain	
Elizabeth Lake	
Lake Sherburne	
Glenns Lake	
Iceberg Lake	

name _____

section _____   date _____

Goals

After completing this lab, you will be able to
- ✓ read a topographic map to answer questions about geographic features.
- ✓ use a map scale to measure distances between locations on the map.
- ✓ use contour lines to determine elevations of unmarked features.

Equipment

calculator
centimeter ruler
drafting dividers

1. Examine the road in the lower left-hand portion of the map. It has a distinctive feature called a "switchback" (hairpin turn), which sometimes appears in roads built on steep slopes. What name has been given to this feature?

_____

Relief is shown by means of *contour lines*. Contour lines indicate areas of equal elevation. If you were to walk along a contour line, you would move neither up nor down. Closely spaced contour lines indicate a steep slope, while widely spaced lines indicate a gentle slope.

When contour lines cross a stream, they tend to bend in the shape of a V. The point of the V is always in the upstream direction. For rivers flowing over relatively level terrain, the V shape may be flattened.

The vertical spacing between contour lines is called the *contour interval* of the map (abbreviated C.I.). A commonly used C.I. is 20 ft, or 5 m for metric maps, but different values are used, depending on the local situation and the map series.

2. What is the C.I. shown on the map?

_____

3. Is this C.I. a large or a small value? Explain.

_____

_____

_____

4. Locate Wynn Mountain. On which side is it steepest? How do you know?

_____

_____

5. Estimate the elevation of its summit, assuming that it is half-way between contour lines.

_____

6. Chief Mountain's elevation is not marked on the map. Using contour lines, estimate the summit's elevation.

_____

7. Canyon Creek is located just to the west of Wynn Mountain. Between what two bodies of water does it flow?

_____

8. Judging by the relative elevation of these two bodies of water, does the water in the creek flow north or south?

_____

name _____

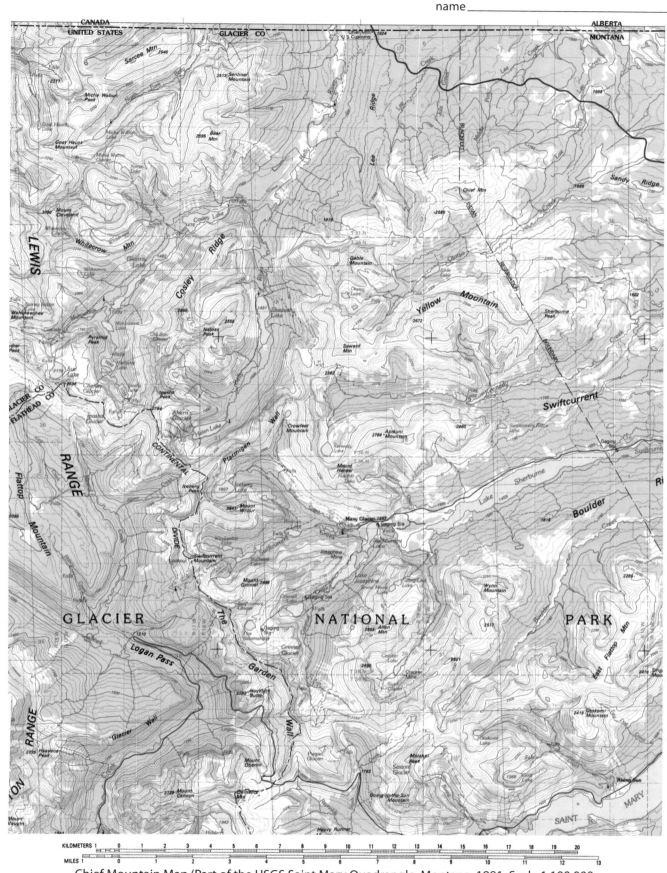

Chief Mountain Map (Part of the USGS Saint Mary Quadrangle, Montana, 1981. Scale 1:100,000;
Contour Interval 50 meters)

8 VOLCANOES AND VOLCANISM

8A Hot Spots

name _____

section _____   date _____

Volcanoes never fail to fascinate us. While most of us will never see an eruption, the world is filled with volcanoes. Some erupt regularly, while others have been quiet for thousands of years. Understanding volcanoes is important for wise dominion, however, since eruptions can cost many lives.

Unlike earthquakes, volcanic eruptions *can* be predicted. When Eyjafjallajökull erupted in Iceland during April of 2010, nobody was surprised. The mountain had been giving warning signs for several months. Volcanoes are found in predictable places too. Your textbook mentions the places where volcanoes are common.

> **Goals**
>
> After completing this lab, you will be able to
> ✓ predict likely locations for volcanic activity.
> ✓ use a GIS system to identify volcanic regions.
> ✓ estimate volcanic distribution and type.

> **Equipment**
>
> computer with Google Earth™

Procedure

1. List the most likely kinds of places to find volcanoes.

_____

_____

_____

Let's see if your ideas are correct. We'll use Google Earth,™ but we must add some extra thematic layers first.

- Start Google Earth.™ Your teacher will give you two KMZ files that add tectonic plate and volcano thematic layers. Load each file by selecting **File | Open** and browsing to the file. Select the file and click **Open**.

- Find the **Temporary Places** checkbox on the left side of the screen and check it. Google Earth™ shows the tectonic plate boundaries as colored lines. Volcanoes are red triangles. To learn more about a volcano, click its triangle. Pick a few volcano symbols and examine the kind of information available.

- Spin the globe and find the places where there are lots of volcanoes. Pay attention to the location and type of tectonic plate boundaries.

Image IBCAO/Image©2011 GeoEye/Data SIO, NOAA, U.S. Navy/GEBCO/©2011 Cnes/Spot Image

Figure 1

2. Which part of the world has the most volcanoes?

_____

_____

3. What does your textbook call this region?

_____

_____

4. Along what kind of plate boundary are these volcanoes found?

_____

_____

5. Look at the eastern coast of Africa. Is there a distinct pattern to the volcanoes in this region? If so, describe it.

_____

_____

6. Do these volcanoes appear to be on a tectonic plate boundary?

_____

7. How do you account for this situation? (*Hint*: Review Chapter 7 Subsection 7.6.)

_____

_____

_____

- **Fly to** the country of Iceland. Examine its volcano distribution.

8. Identify the kind of tectonic plate boundaries Iceland overlies.

_____

9. Count the volcanoes in Iceland. Include any nearby ocean or island volcanoes. How many are there?

_____

- Let's find out how "dense" volcanoes are in Iceland. We need to know how many square kilometers there are for each volcano. So we must find the approximate area of Iceland.

- Measuring the area of an irregular landform can be difficult. We're going to approximate the area with a rectangle.

10. How do you calculate the area of a rectangle?

_____

_____

- Measure the length and width of Iceland with the **Ruler** tool. Measure the most rectangular part of the island. Calculate the area in square kilometers.

11. What is Iceland's approximate area?

_____

12. Based upon your data, how dense are the volcanoes? (*Hint*: Calculate how many square kilometers there are for each volcano.)

_____

13. Now go to the western United States and count the number of volcanoes. Do not count ones off the coast. How many are there?

_____

- Using the rectangle method, estimate the area of the volcanic section of the United States.

14. What is the approximate area of the western United States?

_____

15. How dense are the volcanoes in the western United States?

_____

16. Based upon density, which location is more volcanic, Iceland or the western United States?

_____

17. According to your textbook, which volcano type is the most common?

_____

- Choose three different volcanic regions of the world. Write the region names in the table below. Randomly select 25 volcanoes in each region and click on their red triangle symbols.
- Look at the **Volcano Type** to identify the volcano. If there is more than one type, choose the first one. Treat a pyroclastic volcano as a cinder cone volcano.

name_____

Image IBCAO/Image©2011 GeoEye/Data SIO, NOAA, U.S. Navy/GEBCO/©2011 Cnes/Spot Image

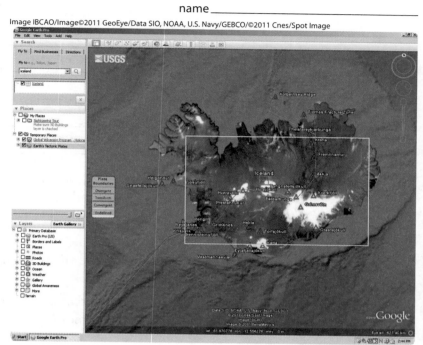

Figure 2 Iceland's approximate area

- Complete the table below by filling in the number of volcanoes of each type.

Region	Shield	Cinder Cone	Stratovolcano	Other

- Now, calculate the percentage of each type. Use the following formula:

$$\% = \frac{\text{\# volcanoes}}{25} \times 100\%.$$

- Write the percentages in parenthesis next to the totals in the table.

18. Based upon your observations, which volcano type is the most common?

_____

8B Volcanic Visits

name_____

section_____ date_____

Unless you happen to live near one, visiting a volcano isn't something you can do for a quick field trip. And even if you could, you probably wouldn't be able to see examples of each type. As your textbook explains, volcanoes come in three major types: shield, cinder cone, and stratovolcano.

Shield volcanoes, such as those in the Hawaiian Islands, are made up entirely of solidified lava flows. In fact, the Hawaiian Islands are composed exclusively of shield volcanoes that have grown upward from the Pacific Ocean floor.

Stratovolcanoes (also known as composite volcanoes) are a combination of shield volcanoes and cinder cones. They are built of layers of lava alternated with layers of cinders and ash (tephra). The Pacific Coast of the United States has a number of composite volcanoes, including Mt. Shasta, Mt. Rainier, Mt. Saint Helens, Mt. Hood, Mt. Lassen, and the volcanic peak in which Crater Lake is located, Mt. Mazama.

Let's do a virtual volcano field trip by exploring two volcanoes. We'll sharpen our map skills as we examine a shield volcano. Then we'll see how a fairly recent eruption from a composite volcano dramatically changed its surroundings.

Goals

After completing this lab, you will be able to
- ✓ use a relief map to explore a typical shield volcano cone.
- ✓ use a map to examine how a recent volcanic eruption affected the volcano's surroundings.

Equipment

centimeter ruler
calculator

Procedure

- Look at the map of Hawaii on page 88. Note the five volcanic peaks: Mauna Kea, 4205 m (13,796 ft); Mauna Loa, 4169 m (13,678 ft); Hualalai, 2521 m (8271 ft); Kohala, 1670 m (5479 ft); and Kilauea, 1248 m (4094 ft). We're going to create a profile map based on a reference line drawn through Mauna Kea.

- The profile will be similar to the one you drew in Lab 7B. However, there will be one difference. The vertical scale will be exaggerated. This technique is often used when profiling certain types of mountains.

- Using the blank grid provided on the map, draw a profile map from west to east (from point *A* to point *B*, a distance of 93 km, or 58 mi) through the summit of Mauna Kea. Points *A* and *B* are both at sea level, so they are placed on the 0 ft contour line.

- Position a ruler parallel to the solid vertical lines.

- Directly below each intersection of line *AB* with a contour line (indicated by a tick mark), mark a point on the profile map grid. Be sure to place the point on the correct elevation line. Each contour line on the map represents 1000 ft, and each line on the profile grid also represents 1000 ft.

- Draw a smooth line connecting the points.

- The profile map's scale (3.5:1) deliberately exaggerates the profile vertically. Let's create a second profile that shows the mountain's true vertical appearance (1:1).

- Divide the elevation of each point by 3.5 and draw a new profile under the first one.

1. Examine the 1:1 profile. What do you conclude about a shield volcano's slope and overall appearance?

_____

_____

2. Examine the 3.5:1 profile. Explain why exaggerating the vertical scale might be useful even though it distorts the mountain's appearance.

_____

_____

- The map of Mt. Saint Helens on page 89 shows some of the effects of the cataclysmic blast of May 18, 1980. Take a few minutes to examine the map, its labeling, and some of the features around the mountain.

3. Compared to the mountain, in what direction or directions did most of the destruction occur?

_____

_____

4. Examine the north rim of the crater. What do you notice about the contour lines?

_____

_____

5. What can you conclude from this shape?

_____

_____

6. Examine the dark gray, *stippled* shading around the mountain. What does it represent?

_____

7. In what direction did this effect occur?

_____

8. Examine the dark gray, *unstippled* shading around the mountain. What does it represent?

_____

9. In what direction did this effect occur?

name_____

_____

- Several new lakes were formed when streams were dammed by debris. These are designated by arrows with a number 3 on them.

10. How many of these features appear on the map?

_____

- The arrow labeled 5 shows several new islands that formed in Spirit Lake at the time of the eruption.

11. Assuming there were no islands in Spirit Lake before the blast, how many new islands were formed?

_____

- Before the eruption, Mt. Saint Helens possessed a picturesque cone-shaped peak. The elevation of its summit was 2950 m.

12. How many meters of height did the mountain lose?

_____

Figure 1 Mt. Saint Helens before and after the 1980 eruption

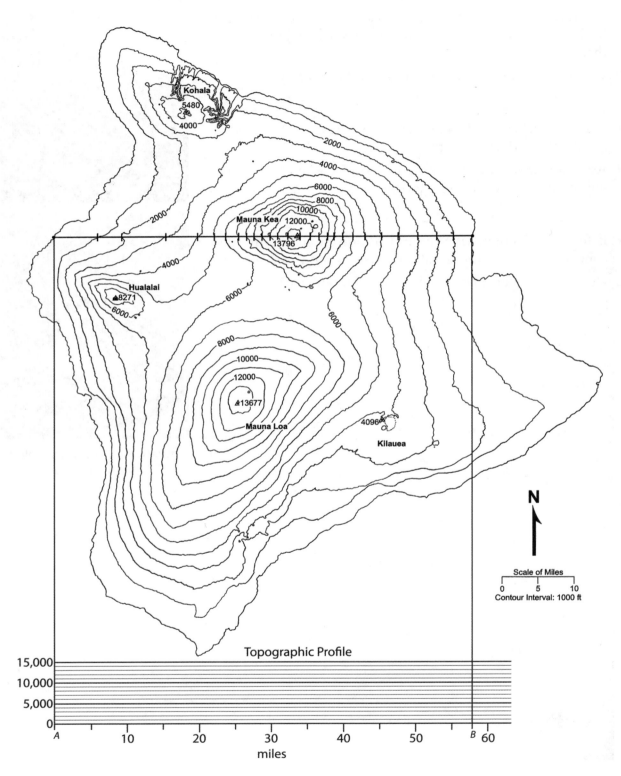

Topographic Profile

Contour map of the Island of Hawaii (based on USGS 1975. Scale 1:250,000)

name_____

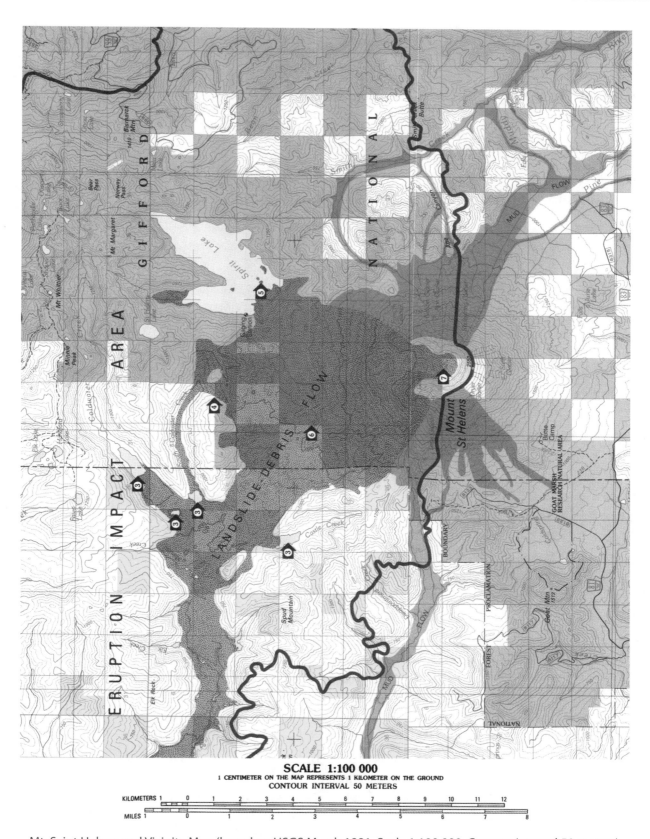

SCALE 1:100 000
1 CENTIMETER ON THE MAP REPRESENTS 1 KILOMETER ON THE GROUND
CONTOUR INTERVAL 50 METERS

Mt. Saint Helens and Vicinity Map (based on USGS March 1981. Scale 1:100,000; Contour Interval 50 meters)

9 MINERALS AND ORES

9A Crafting a Crystal

When you hear the word *crystal*, what comes to mind? Do you see a mental image of a sparkling gemstone? Or perhaps a giant chunk of quartz? Crystals come in a vast array of colors, sizes, and types.

Back in Chapter 2 of your textbook, you learned that crystals are made from regular, repeating patterns of particles (atoms or molecules). In many crystals, this structure creates the regular, flat faces that we usually associate with crystals. In some materials, such as metals, the crystalline structure is too small to see.

Minerals are natural crystal structures made from inorganic substances. Under the right conditions, solutions of these substances "grow" into crystals. In this lab you will be able to watch crystals form in just a few days.

Procedure

- Add 100 mL of water to the saucepan and bring it to a boil on the hot plate. Once it boils, remove the pan from the burner and place it on a heatproof surface.

- Slowly stir the sugar into the hot water. Continue to add sugar until no more will dissolve.

- Add a drop of food coloring to color the solution.

- Pour the solution into a clean glass beaker. Do *not* include any of the undissolved sugar.

- Tie one end of a string around a pencil. Lay the pencil across the beaker, with the end of the string dangling down into the sugar solution. Adjust the string until the end is at least 2 cm above the bottom of the beaker.

- Put the beaker in a place where it will be undisturbed for several days. Avoid direct sunlight or heat sources.

- Repeat the above steps using alum and then Epsom salts. Be sure to rinse the pan and spoon each time so you don't contaminate the solutions.

- After several days, remove each string and allow the crystals to dry. Observe the crystals with the hand magnifier. Draw the shape of each crystal in the spaces on page 92.

Do *not* taste the sugar crystals since they were not produced under food-safe conditions!

name _____

section _____   date _____

Goals

After completing this lab, you will be able to

✓ explain what a crystal is and how it forms.

✓ grow crystals in a supersaturated solution.

✓ examine and draw crystal shapes.

Equipment

saucepan
hot plate or stove
white sugar (sucrose), 200 g
alum (potassium or ammonium aluminum sulfate), 100 g
Epsom salts (magnesium sulfate heptahydrate), 100 g
food coloring
spoon or stirring rod
beakers, 250 mL (3)
pencils (3)
cotton strings, 15 cm (3)
hand magnifier

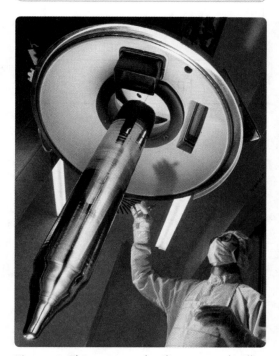

Figure 1 This man-made silicon crystal will eventually become integrated circuits like the ones in your computer.

Sugar

Alum

Epsom Salts

1. As each solution cools, it is said to be *supersaturated*. What do you think this term means?

_____

_____

2. Why do you think the solution is supersaturated when cool but not supersaturated when hot?

_____

_____

3. In a few sentences describe what you think happened during the days when the crystals "grew" on the string.

_____

_____

_____

4. Did just one crystal form?

_____

5. When you stir sugar into a drink such as tea or coffee, it disappears. What happens to it?

_____

_____

_____

6. How could you re-crystallize the sugar stirred into a cup of tea?

_____

_____

7. Based upon the definition of a mineral, explain why sugar crystals are *not* an example of a mineral.

_____

_____

_____

8. Evaluate the following statement and explain why it's true or false: "All minerals are crystals and all crystals are minerals."

name_____

_____

_____

_____

_____

_____

9. Why is it valuable for humans to grow man-made crystals?

_____

_____

_____

_____

_____

9B Unmasking Mysterious Minerals

name_____

section_____ date_____

Minerals are naturally occurring, inorganic, crystalline solids that form the building blocks of rocks. Scientists have identified over three thousand different minerals! But how do scientists classify minerals? And how do they tell them apart when they look almost alike?

Obviously, they use their senses to gather data from mineral specimens. As you learned in Lab 2A, we call this kind of data *descriptive data*. But descriptive data depends to some degree upon the observer.

Whenever possible, scientists prefer *measured data* collected by instruments since it's much less subjective. As it turns out, scientists classify and identify minerals by a combination of both descriptive and measured data. In this lab, you'll examine several common minerals and collect both kinds of data. Let's get started!

Procedure

- Examine the table shown on page 98. The first column contains a list of the minerals you'll be examining. The next four columns are for descriptive data, while the last two are for measured data. If a box is shaded, you won't be collecting that kind of data for the mineral.

- A mineral's *color* refers to the appearance of the mineral in ordinary light. Record the color of each mineral in the "Color" column.

- A mineral's *streak* is the color of the powdered mineral. If you rub a softer mineral against a streak plate or unglazed ceramic tile, it will leave a colored mark. Perform the streak test on each mineral that has an unshaded box in the "Streak" column.

- A mineral's *luster* is a rating of how it reflects light. If a mineral looks like metal, it has a *metallic* luster. If it is shiny like glass, it has a *vitreous* luster. If it isn't shiny and doesn't look like metal, it has a *dull* luster. Record the luster of each mineral that has an unshaded box in the "Luster" column in the table.

- Next, test each mineral for magnetic properties. A magnetic mineral will be attracted to a magnet. In the "Magnetic?" column, record a *Y* for magnetic minerals and an *N* for nonmagnetic ones.

Goals

After completing this lab, you will be able to

✓ describe a mineral's identifying properties.

✓ estimate a mineral's hardness.

✓ measure a mineral's specific gravity.

✓ use descriptive and measured data to build a mineral characteristics table.

Equipment

rock and mineral collection
streak plate or unglazed ceramic tile
pre-1983 penny
steel knife
glass plate
beaker, 250 mL or larger
thread
ring stand
spring balance
magnet

The first measured data test we'll be collecting is *hardness*. As your textbook explains, minerals are rated by the Mohs Hardness Scale. In this test, common objects are used to scratch mineral specimens. If the object can scratch the mineral, the mineral must be softer than the object. If the object can't scratch the mineral, the mineral must be harder. We're going to use a fingernail (hardness of 2½), a copper penny (hardness of 3½), a steel knife blade (hardness of 5–5½), and a glass plate (hardness of 5½). The following table identifies the guidelines for each hardness value.

Mohs Hardness Number	
1	can easily be scratched with the fingernail
2	can barely be scratched with the fingernail
3	cannot be scratched with the fingernail but can be scratched with a penny
4	cannot be scratched with a penny but can be scratched easily with a steel knife blade
5	can barely be scratched with a steel knife blade
6	cannot be scratched with a steel knife blade but is hard enough to scratch glass
7	can easily scratch a steel knife blade and glass

You can test the hardness of a mineral by trying to scratch it with the softest test object (the fingernail) first and then working upward through the harder objects. Once you succeed in scratching the mineral, stop. When testing whether a mineral will scratch the glass plate, do *not* hold the glass plate in your hands. Keep it flat on a table. Draw the mineral firmly across the glass just once. If you think you have scratched the glass, see whether you can rub off the scratch mark with your finger. If it comes off, the mineral did *not* scratch the glass. A true scratch mark will remain.

- Determine as nearly as you can the hardness of each of the minerals that has an unshaded box in the "Hardness" column of the table. If a mineral's hardness appears to be in between two numbers, you may record the hardness as halfway between two values (for example, 2½).

Another kind of measured data is a mineral's *specific gravity*. Specific gravity is the ratio between the mineral's density and water's density. To measure specific gravity, a thread is tied to the specimen and it is hung from a spring scale. The specimen is weighed. It is then submerged in a beaker full of water without letting the mineral touch the bottom. The mineral weighs less when submerged because of the buoyant force of the water. We calculate specific gravity with the following formula:

$$\text{s.g.} = \frac{\text{weight in air (g)}}{\text{weight in air (g)} - \text{weight in water (g)}}.$$

Figure 1 Testing hardness with a glass plate

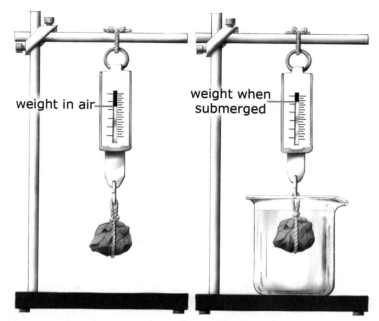

weight in air

weight when submerged

Figure 2

- Determine the specific gravity of each of the minerals that has an unshaded box. Record your measurements and calculations in the calculation space below the table. Record your final results in the "S.G." column of the table.

1. Based upon what you've learned in this lab, explain how a geologist would go about identifying an unknown mineral sample.

   _____

   _____

   _____

2. Are all the minerals in your collection naturally occurring, or are some of them man-made? Explain.

   _____

   _____

3. All of the streak tests you performed were for relatively soft materials. How would you perform a streak test for a mineral whose hardness is 8½?

   _____

   _____

4. What is the relationship of minerals to rocks?

   _____

   _____

5. Some of the minerals in the collection are called ores; others are not. What do you suppose is the difference between them?

_____

_____

6. In a few sentences, explain the value of being able to identify minerals.

_____

_____

_____

_____

Mineral	Color	Streak	Luster	Magnetic?	Hardness	S. G.
bauxite (ore)						
magnetite						
chalcopyrite						
microcline						
galena						
milky quartz						
gypsum						
pyrite						
hematite						
rose quartz						
calcite						
corundum						
fluorite						
muscovite						

**Galena contains lead, a toxic metal. Do not eat or drink during this lab.
Be sure to wash your hands and work surface when you're finished.**

Calculations

10 ROCKS

10A Rock-Solid Science

name_____

section_____   date_____

Rocks are the materials of which the earth's crust is made. In Lab 9B you studied some important rock-building minerals. You also did a series of tests to classify them and confirm their identity. As you discovered, scientists use a mixture of descriptive and measured data to build an understanding of each mineral.

You learned in your textbook that scientists divide rocks into three major categories: *igneous*, *sedimentary*, and *metamorphic*. Each type forms under different conditions. In fact, the way a rock forms determines its appearance and physical properties.

In this lab you'll be examining about two dozen rock specimens taken from the three major rock types. We'll explore some of the ways rocks are tested and identified. Keep your textbook handy. It will help you answer questions about certain rocks. Also, don't forget to check Appendixes J and K!

Goals

After completing this lab, you will be able to

✓ examine samples from each major rock type and describe their defining characteristics.

✓ perform common tests on rock samples.

Equipment

rock and mineral collection
hand magnifier
beaker, 250 mL or larger
dilute hydrochloric acid (2 *M*)
eyedropper
paper towels

Procedure

- Study the seven specimens of igneous rocks in your collection (#8–14).

1. List the igneous rocks that are light colored. These rocks have a high silica content.

_____

2. List the rocks that are dark colored (black or dark gray). These rocks have a low silica content.

_____

3. Which two specimens are coarse grained? These are igneous rocks that formed from certain kinds of magma under conditions that permitted the formation of large, visible crystals.

_____

4. Which of these two has a porphyritic texture (some large grains in a matrix of smaller crystals)?

_____

5. How many different minerals appear to make up granite? (*Hint*: Count the number of different colors within the rock.)

_____

6. Which specimens have a porous structure? These are volcanic rocks that have bubble holes created by trapped gases.

_____

Figure 1 Rocky variety: how do we tell them all apart?

7. Test your pumice specimen to see if it floats on water. Many specimens are less dense than water. Does it float?

_____

8. Which rock exhibits the best example of conchoidal fracture? This rock was formed from magma or lava that contained no dissolved gases. (*Hint*: See Figure 9-10 in your textbook.)

_____

• Study the seven specimens of sedimentary rocks in your collection (#23–29).

9. Which of the samples shows the best evidence of layering (stratification)?

_____

• Dip each of the seven specimens into a beaker of water.

10. Do any exhibit an earthy smell? Which one(s)?

_____

• Dry your specimens with a paper towel. Place them in a row on a clean paper towel. Using the eyedropper, place a single drop of dilute hydrochloric acid on each one. You should wear eye protection when working with acids.

11. Which ones effervesce (fizz)?

_____

The so-called "acid test" reveals the presence of minerals based on carbonate compounds. These are compounds made from metal ions combined with carbon-oxygen ions. When the acid comes in contact with a carbonate, it reacts, creating carbon dioxide gas, water, and a salt. Certain sedimentary and metamorphic rocks as well as some minerals contain carbonates.

• After you have finished testing each specimen, rinse the acid from it under a *gently* running faucet. Dry the samples with a paper towel.

12. Examine your conglomerate rock specimen. What color is the matrix (the natural "cement" that binds together the fragments making up the rock)?

_____

13. Note the wide range in the sizes of the fragments within the conglomerate. Are the fragments interlocking or separate?

_____

14. List any of the sedimentary rocks that are porous.

_____

15. Which type of rock might be useful as a source of petroleum?

name_____

_____

• Study the eight specimens of metamorphic rocks in your collection (#15–22).

16. From which rock was gneiss probably formed? What about slate? quartzite? marble?

_____

_____

17. List any of your specimens that exhibit foliation.

_____

• Dip each of the eight specimens into a beaker of water.

18. Identify any that exhibit an earthy smell.

_____

• Dry your specimens with a paper towel. Place them in a row on a clean paper towel. Using the eyedropper, place a single drop of dilute hydrochloric acid on each one. You should wear eye protection when working with acids.

19. List any that effervesce.

_____

• After you have finished testing each specimen, rinse the acid from it under a *gently* running faucet. Dry the samples with a paper towel.

20. Name one physical property that scientists use to identify minerals that could also be useful in identifying rocks.

_____

21. Which physical properties that are useful for identifying minerals are *not* useful for identifying rocks?

_____

_____

22. Why aren't these properties appropriate for identifying rocks?

_____

_____

23. Which of the three major classes of rocks exhibits true stratification?

_____

24. What evidence suggests that slate might be related to shale?

_____

_____

25. What evidence suggests that marble and limestone are chemically similar?

_____

_____

26. Which of your metamorphic rocks did you observe to be nonfoliated?

_____

10B Geological Speed Bumps

name_____

section_____   date_____

Back in Chapter 5, you learned one way that some scientists try to describe the earth's history: the *geologic column*. Using an old-earth model, they assume that the layers of rock we find today were laid down over a long period of time, about 4.5 billion years.

Regrettably, there is no single place on Earth where geologists can find a complete sequence of all the layers. So old-earth geologists have pieced together many different observations to create a picture of what they think a complete geologic column would look like. Page 103 in your textbook shows this.

Geologists obtain the dates for the rock layers from two sources: *radiometric dating* and *fossils*. As your textbook explains, deep-time radiometric dating is unreliable. The other method, fossil dating, rests on two key assumptions.

The first assumption old-earth geologists make is that rock layers are stacked in order. The deepest layer is the oldest, while the top layer is the youngest. This idea is called the *principle of superposition*.

Second, geologists choose certain fossils to date rocks. They use species whose age they believe they know. These are called *index fossils*. When those fossils appear in rock layers, they assume the rock is the same age as the fossils. If layers of index-fossil-bearing rock are separated by a middle layer, they assume the middle layer was formed during the time period between that of the outer layers.

In this lab, we're going to examine the fossil dating method to see how well it works. We'll also take a look at some controversial evidence and decide if we should use it in support of the young-earth model.

Goals

After completing this lab, you will be able to

✓ identify examples of problems in the geologic time scale.

✓ analyze the reasoning in relating the geologic column and fossil record.

✓ examine possible interpretations of "out-of-place" human artifacts in geologic strata.

Equipment

Figure 1 Ammonites are popular index fossils.

Procedure

• Examine the geologic column chart on page 103. Note the various time divisions and subdivisions (*eon*, *era*, *period*, and *epoch*).

1. In what eon and era is the Carboniferous period?

_____

2. When did the Carboniferous period supposedly end?

_____

• Examine the list at the top of the next page. It shows a series of discoveries that appear to contradict the basic principles of the geologic column. Each item includes two geologic time periods. Make a note of these!

• Draw short vertical lines on the chart to indicate the position of the two times. Then draw a horizontal line with arrowheads at each end in between the vertical lines. Label the horizontal line with a short description of the discovery.

Figure 2 The Carboniferous period is named for the coal that old-earth geologists believe was laid down during this period.

- Add each item to the chart until you've marked them all. The first example has been completed for you.

Discovery 1. Gymnosperm pollen was found in the Grand Canyon in the lowest strata (Precambrian), even though these plants supposedly first appeared in the Permian period.

Discovery 2. Fossil wood was found embedded in Precambrian rock in northern Quebec, Canada. Two radiocarbon dating tests on samples of the wood gave ages of about 4000 years (Holocene epoch).

Discovery 3. Cambrian and early Carboniferous layers that alternate back and forth (two complete cycles) were found in one part of the north rim of the Grand Canyon.

Discovery 4. Chief Mountain in Glacier National Park in Montana consists of Precambrian rock on top of Cretaceous rock. Fossils are therefore out of order.

Discovery 5. A dinosaur bone from the late Cretaceous period contained soft tissue (possibly blood vessels and blood cells). Scientists were surprised that unfossilized soft tissue could survive longer than a million years.

Discovery 6. An iron pot was found embedded in Carboniferous period coal. Metal human artifacts supposedly exist only in the Holocene epoch.

Discoveries 7 and 8. Your teacher may provide other examples for you to mark on the chart.

3. Based upon Discoveries 1–5, does the fossil dating method appear to be reliable? Explain why or why not.

_____

_____

_____

4. Do Discoveries 1–5 create any problems for the young-earth model? Explain your answer.

_____

_____

_____

5. Old-earth geologists use index fossils to establish ages for rock layers. Other scientists then use the rock layer ages to date new fossil discoveries made in these layers. Is this method logical? Explain.

_____

_____

_____

Discovery 6 is an example of an *out-of-place artifact* (OOPart). These are man-made objects that are found in "pre-human" geologic formations. They are therefore "problems" because they supposedly shouldn't be where they are found. Many OOParts have been found, including pots, gold chains, metal tools, nails, and figurines.

Sadly, almost all OOParts have been discovered by accident rather than from excavations conducted by professional scientists under properly documented conditions. Most secular and Christian scientists consider them to be of questionable value as evidence.

One of the marks of a good scientist is identifying all possible explanations for evidence that appears to contradict current ideas. You should try to develop this quality as a student scientist. Let's use OOParts as an exercise to refine our thinking skills.

name_____

Figure 3 OOParts like this hammer are sometimes used as evidence against the geologic column.

6. List three possible explanations for OOParts that are acceptable to a biblical worldview.

_____

_____

_____

_____

7. Some people use OOParts as evidence that the earth is young. Since very few OOPart finds have been properly documented, however, should they be used in this way? Why or why not?

_____

_____

_____

_____

8. If a scientifically conducted archaeological expedition were to excavate a genuine OOPart from Precambrian rock, how would an old-earth geologist most likely explain the object? Assume that the object is genuine and its discovery is properly documented. Also assume that there is no way that the object could have been accidentally incorporated into the rock at a later date.

_____

_____

_____

9. How would a young-earth geologist most likely explain the object?

_____

_____

Eon	Era	Period	Epoch		Discovery									Millions of years before the present
					1	2	3	4	5	6	7	8		

Eon	Era	Period	Epoch
Phanerozoic	Cenozoic	Quaternary	Recent (Holocene)
			Pleistocene
		Tertiary	Pliocene
			Miocene
			Oligocene
			Eocene
			Paleocene
	Mesozoic	Cretaceous	
		Jurassic	
		Triassic	
	Paleozoic	Permian	
		Carboniferous	
		Devonian	
		Silurian	
		Ordovician	
		Cambrian	
Precambrian	Proterozoic		
	Archean		
	Hadean Time		

Pollen in Grand Canyon

Millions of years before the present:
0.01
1.6
5.3
23.7
35.6
56.8
66.4
144
208
245
286
320
365
408
438
520
555
2500
3800
4600

11 Fossils

name ____________________

section ____________ date ____________

11A How Old Is It?

"How old are you?" That's the first thing small children ask each other when they meet. But knowing something's age isn't important just to children. It's even more important to scientists and historians. So we shouldn't be surprised when scientists try to come up with better ways of dating things.

One of the most popular methods of dating organic material (material that once was alive) is *radiocarbon dating*. This method works by measuring the amount of a special kind of carbon called ^{14}C contained within the material.

There are several kinds of carbon atoms in the atmosphere, but ^{14}C is special because it is radioactive and changes into nitrogen over time at a very specific rate. This process is called *radioactive decay*. Living things absorb ^{14}C from the atmosphere or from their food as long as they're alive. Once they die, they stop absorbing it, and the ^{14}C within their structure begins to change to nitrogen.

Scientists date an organic object (or things made from organic materials) by measuring the amount of ^{14}C it contains. They compare this quantity to the amount of ^{14}C believed to be in the atmosphere at the time the living material died. From these numbers, they try to estimate the object's age.

Goals

After completing this lab, you will be able to

- ✓ describe the key steps in radiocarbon dating.
- ✓ examine radiocarbon accuracy using historical dates.
- ✓ explain why calibration is needed for accurate radiocarbon dating.
- ✓ identify valid and invalid uses of radiocarbon dating.

Equipment

graph paper (provided)

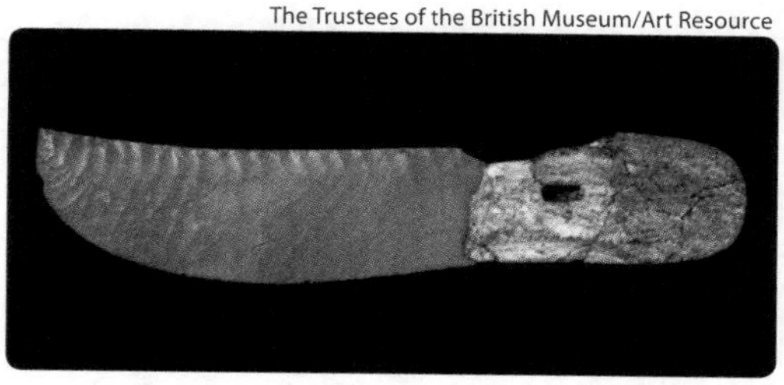

Figure 1 Radiocarbon dating works only with organic materials or objects made from organic materials (in this case, the knife's ivory handle).

Procedure

- Examine the graph below. It shows how the amount of ^{14}C decays (decreases) from 100% at the time of the living material's death to smaller amounts over time.

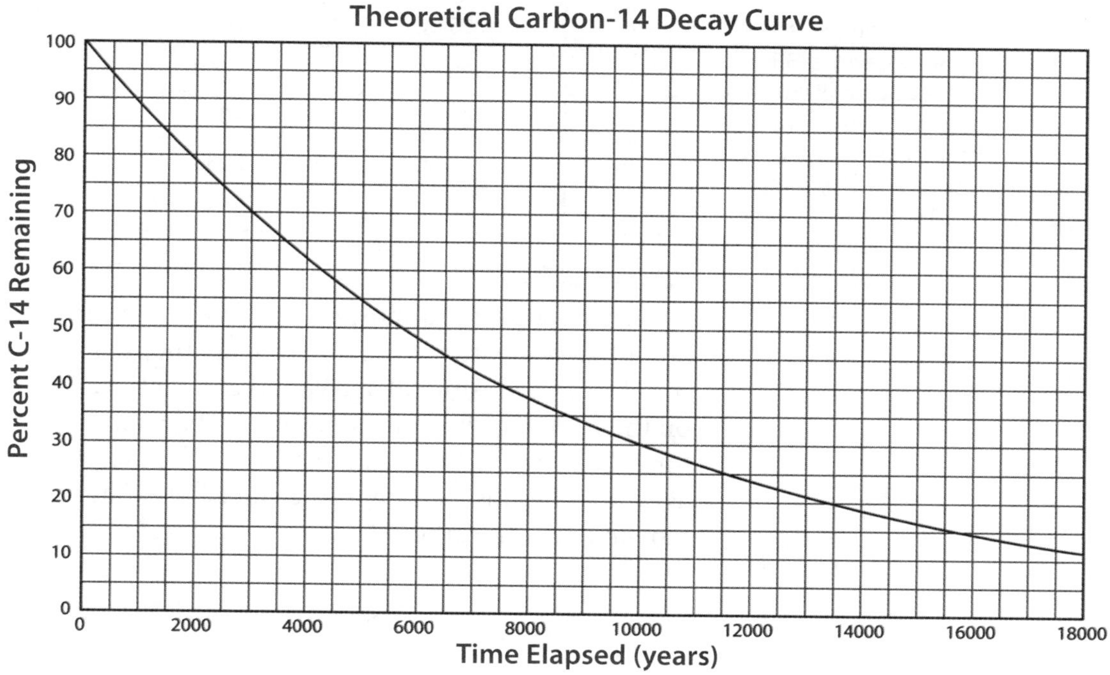
Theoretical Carbon-14 Decay Curve
Percent C-14 Remaining
100
90
80
70
60
50
40
30
20
10
0
0
2000
4000
6000
8000
10000
12000
14000
16000
18000
Time Elapsed (years)

1. If a sample contains 90% of the ¹⁴C it contained at death, how many years have passed?

_____

2. If a sample contains 50% of the ¹⁴C it contained at death, how many years have passed?

_____

Due to many other factors, radiocarbon dating is actually much more complicated than these two examples suggest. When you analyze a sample, you obtain an actual count of the ¹⁴C atoms present, not the percentage of the original atoms still remaining. In order to calculate the percentage, you need to know how many ¹⁴C atoms were in the sample at the time of death. This amount depends upon the amount of ¹⁴C in the *atmosphere* at that same time. However, we don't know this value! That's why radiocarbon dating can be difficult. Let's explore how scientists try to solve this problem.

The table below shows the results of a radiocarbon test conducted on ten of the Dead Sea Scrolls. In each case, archaeologists were confident that they knew the age of each scroll from historical data. So their historical dates make it possible to check the radiocarbon ages for accuracy.

What's a BP?

Look at the third and fourth columns of the table. Instead of the familiar BC or AD dates, these numbers are in "years BP." What's BP? It stands for "Before Present." In the world of radiocarbon dating, the "present" is defined as AD 1950. Why 1950? That's the year scientists started using radiocarbon dating. All dates are therefore referenced to this year. To convert a BC date to a BP age, we just add the years BC to 1950. Now we have the object's age as of 1950. Of course, to obtain its age today, we just add on the number of years that have passed since 1950.

Sample	Historical Date	Historical Age (years BP)	Radiocarbon Age (years BP)
1	25 BC	1975	2094
2	30 BC	1980	2054
3	63 BC	2013	2044
4	75 BC	2025	1954
5	88 BC	2038	2041
6	90 BC	2040	1984
7	100 BC	2050	1823
8	100 BC	2050	1964
9	138 BC	2088	2141
10	200 BC	2150	2095

"Radiocarbon Dating of Scrolls and Linen Fragments from the Judean Desert" by A. J. Timothy Jull, et al., from *Radiocarbon* Vol. 37, No. 1. Copyright © 1995 A. J. Timothy Jull. From the Department of Geosciences, The University of Arizona and the University of Arizona Libraries.

Let's assume the atmospheric ¹⁴C has been constant throughout all of Earth's history. If this were true, the radiocarbon age of the scroll and the historical age would be identical. The graph shown on the next page illustrates this idea. The *x*-axis represents the historical age, while the *y*-axis represents the *theoretical* radiocarbon age. The graph is a straight line since both dates match. Now let's plot *actual* radiocarbon data!

name_____

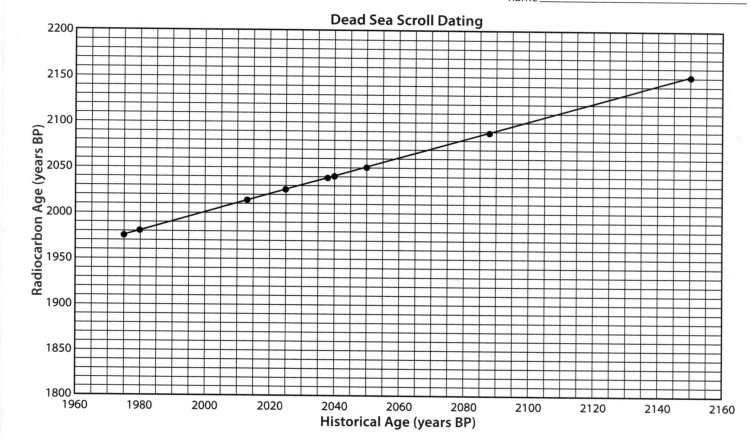

Dead Sea Scroll Dating

- Plot each actual radiocarbon age (the fourth column of the table) on the same graph. Attempt to draw a smooth curve that moves only upward or downward between the points.

3. Is the plot almost identical to the theoretical radiocarbon plot?

_____

4. Is the plot a straight (or almost straight) line?

_____

What you are seeing is variation between the actual and theoretical radiocarbon ages. Shortly after scientists started using radiocarbon dating, they realized that the atmospheric ^{14}C *hasn't* been constant throughout the earth's history. Many factors can change it. Fluctuations in the cosmic rays coming from space can increase or decrease it. Climate changes and variations in ocean flow patterns can affect local ^{14}C levels. Different parts of the world also vary from each other. In the 1950s and 1960s, nuclear weapons tests almost doubled the ^{14}C in the atmosphere!

5. Despite these limitations, could radiocarbon dating still be useful? Explain why or why not.

_____

_____

_____

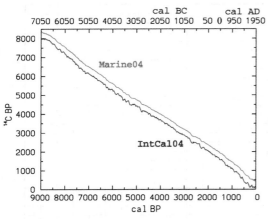

Figure 2 Scientists use calibration curves to improve the accuracy of radiocarbon dating.

Scientists realized that they could improve radiocarbon dating by "tweaking" the theoretical curve. They could use historical dates that they knew and "bend" the theoretical radiocarbon curve to match. This process is called *calibration*.

Scientists often use calibration curves to adjust things that don't behave exactly as theory says they should. The graph you made could be turned into a very simple calibration curve. Real calibration curves contain far more data points, however. All modern radiocarbon dating labs use calibration curves to improve their accuracy.

6. Can radiocarbon dating be used to find the age of rocks from the Grand Canyon? Why or why not?

_____

_____

7. A scientist uses radiocarbon dating to find the age of an ancient piece of cloth. The age is 12,100 years BP. Based upon a biblical worldview, explain why this number can't be correct.

_____

_____

_____

8. You read an article that discusses the age of a human skeleton excavated by an archaeologist. The calibrated radiocarbon age is 4000 years BP. The archaeologist believes the skeleton to be no older than 3500 years BP. Based upon a biblical worldview, should you reject the radiocarbon age?

_____

_____

The calibration curves scientists use today are not based on dated historical objects. Instead, they are based on tree rings, corals, ocean sediments, and ice cores. Scientists claim these calibration curves make reliable dating back to 26,000 years BP possible.

9. From a biblical worldview, explain why calibration curves cannot extend radiocarbon dating back this far.

_____

_____

11B Trilobite-ology

name _____

section _____ date _____

A common and easily recognized kind of fossil is a trilobite. Trilobite bodies consist of three lobes arranged side by side along their length, hence the name, *tri-lobite*. Trilobites are members of the animal phylum Arthropoda (just like insects, spiders, shrimps, and crabs) because they have exoskeletons and jointed appendages. In fact, some trilobites look very similar to modern young horseshoe crabs. However, there are no known living trilobites today, so they are considered extinct. All that we know about trilobites has come from studying their fossils and making educated guesses by comparing them with living arthropods. Let's do some "trilobite-ology" by studying trilobite diagrams and fossils.

Procedure

- Study Diagram A below. Notice the raised center lobe that runs from the head through the tail. Two sections are on either side of the center lobe and are separated from it by the longitudinal (long-wise) axial furrows. Trilobites get their name from these three longitudinal lobes.

- The body can also be divided into three sections: *head* (or *cephalon*), *thorax*, and *tail* (or *pygidium*). Often only one of the sections will have been preserved in a fossil. This is because, like most marine arthropods, trilobites molted their exoskeletons as they grew. So many trilobite fossils are just pieces of the shed exoskeleton.

- Notice the eyes and variously shaped sections of the cephalon. The size, shape, and position of these parts are helpful for identifying different trilobite species.

1. How many smaller segments (*pleura*) are there in the thorax?

_____

- Gills were attached to two pairs of legs, used for swimming or crawling, under each of these segments. The number of segments in the thorax is used to help identify different species of trilobites.

- Observe that the pygidium is also made up of several sections. However, these segments apparently grew together to form an inflexible plate.

- Now study Diagram B on page 113. You should notice that although it is definitely a trilobite, the size, shape, position, and number of the various parts are different from the ones in Diagram A. Label Diagram B using the same terms used in Diagram A. Have your teacher check your work before you proceed further.

Goals

After completing this lab, you will be able to
✓ identify the various structural parts of a trilobite.
✓ determine the subgroup to which particular trilobites belong.

Equipment

trilobite fossils (1 or more)
hand magnifier

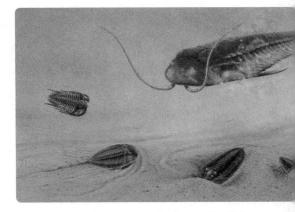

Figure 1 Trilobites weren't always fossils!

Diagram A

marginal furrow   glabella

facial suture

free cheek

eye

fixed cheek

genal spine

pleura

axial furrow

head

thorax

tail

left lobe   center lobe   right lobe

- Observe Diagrams C, D, E, and F on the next page. Note the size indicated along the left side of each one. Some trilobites were up to 72 cm long, whereas others were as small as 1 mm. While each differs in *morphology* (structure), they were all trilobites. The fossil record indicates that there were over 17,000 species of trilobites!

- Examine your trilobite fossil (or fossils) with the hand magnifier. Remember, your fossil may not be complete.

2. Which sections are present in your fossil?

_____

_____

- If the cephalon region is present, examine the eyes.

3. Are the eyes simple or compound? (*Hint*: Look at a picture of an insect's eyes for comparison. Insects have compound eyes.)

_____

4. Does it have a genal spine?

_____

5. Do you think your fossil is of a molted exoskeleton or of the whole organism? Explain why.

_____

_____

- If there is much rock with your fossil, you may find fossils of additional trilobites or other organisms.

6. Are there other fossils present? If so, what do you think they are?

_____

_____

7. Many living arthropods experience changes in the shape of their bodies each time they molt. Assuming that this also occurred with trilobites, how does this fact affect the conclusions you made about your fossil?

_____

_____

_____

- On a separate sheet of paper, draw your trilobite as if it were flat. Include as much detail as possible. Be careful not to add details that you cannot see. Label the parts.

name_____

Diagram B

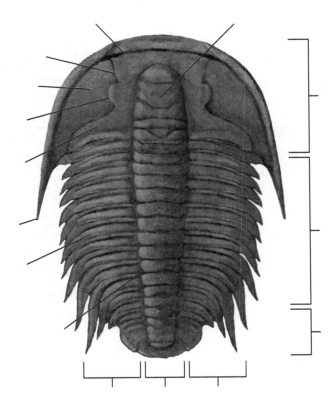

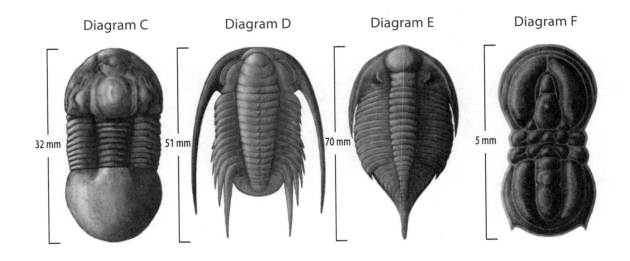

Diagram C   Diagram D   Diagram E   Diagram F

32 mm   51 mm   70 mm   5 mm

• There are three to nine orders in the subphylum Trilobita, depending on the characteristics used for classification. Five of the orders included in most classifications are listed below. Read the description of each subgroup and decide to which subgroup the trilobites in Diagrams C–F belong. Place the correct subgroup name in the blank below each diagram.

Order	Description
Agnostida	small, total body length is 13 mm or less; 2–3 thoracic segments; blind (no eyes); no facial sutures
Redlichiida	large semicircular cephalon with genal spines; numerous thoracic segments (up to 44); crescent-shaped eyes; small pygidium
Corynexochida	large semicircular cephalon, usually with spines; 5–11 thoracic segments; pygidium nearly the same size as the cephalon or only slightly smaller; eyes generally elongated
Phacopida	facial sutures extend from the front of the cephalon, to the eyes, to the rear of the shield; 8–19 thoracic segments; large- to medium-size pygidium
Ptychopariida	more than three thoracic segments; eyes present or absent; blunt pleural spines (Any that do not fit the other descriptions fall into this order.)

8. What can we learn from living animals that fossils cannot tell us?

_____

_____

_____

12 WEATHERING, EROSION, AND SOILS

12A All Worn Out

name _____

section _____   date _____

Nothing seems more durable than rocks. They look like they'll last forever! But rocks can be surprisingly fragile. Under the right conditions, they can wear away in very little time. This process is called *weathering*.

As you learned in your textbook, there are several different kinds of weathering. In this lab, we're going to look at *chemical weathering*. Chemical weathering occurs when acids weaken and break down certain kinds of rock.

1. What kinds of rocks are most likely to be affected by acids? (*Hint*: Think back to Lab 10A.)

_____

_____

_____

2. Chemical weathering can happen quickly or slowly. List three things that you think might speed it up.

_____

_____

Let's do some chemical weathering of our own. We're going to start with a fairly weak acid (acetic acid), although it's stronger than the natural carbonic acid that is responsible for most chemical weathering.

Goals

After completing this lab, you will be able to
✓ describe the chemical processes involved in chemical weathering.
✓ determine what speeds up chemical weathering.
✓ explain how chemical weathering could have helped form some caves.

Equipment

beakers,100 mL (4)
laboratory scale (accurate to 0.1 g)
microwave oven
limestone or marble pebbles (4)
white vinegar
dilute hydrochloric acid (2 *M*)
eye protection
hot mitt or pot holder
lab apron
hammer
old dishtowel
plastic spoons

Procedure

• Your teacher has given you four limestone or marble pebbles. Wrap one of the pebbles in the towel. On a hard, sturdy surface like the floor or a hard countertop, use the hammer to break it into several pieces. (Do *not* pulverize the pebble.) Breaking the pebble increases its exposed surface area.

• Measure the mass of each of the unbroken pebbles using the laboratory scale. Round the mass to the nearest 0.1 g and record it in the "Mass Before" column of the table on page 117. Measure the mass of all the broken pebble pieces and record it as well.

• Fill three beakers with 75 mL of white vinegar.

• Place one beaker in a microwave oven and heat the vinegar to just below boiling. Use care and wear hand protection when removing the hot beaker from the microwave!

Figure 1 What controls the speed of chemical weathering?

Figure 2 Rapid chemical weathering can be dramatic!

Figure 3 Before and after

- Place a pebble in one of the beakers of room-temperature vinegar. Place a second pebble in the beaker of hot vinegar. Place the broken pebble pieces in the other beaker of room-temperature vinegar. Make a note of the time.

While the pebbles experience chemical weathering, we're going to explore chemical weathering with a stronger acid. As you'll learn in Chapter 17, some scientists believe acids may have helped form certain types of caves.

- Under your teacher's supervision, carefully fill the fourth beaker with 50 mL of dilute hydrochloric acid. Handle this acid with care. Wear eye and clothing protection.

- Place the beaker on a chemical-resistant surface. Using a spoon, carefully add the fourth pebble to the acid. It should begin to fizz vigorously as it reacts with the acid. Do *not* lean over the beaker since the reaction generates a fine acid mist above the surface. This mist can burn your eyes, nose, and throat!

- Allow the reaction to continue for five minutes. Then, using the spoon, carefully remove the pebble from the acid. Rinse it under cold running water and dry it with a paper towel. Do not touch the pebble with your hands until it has been thoroughly rinsed!

- The acid mist may have settled on the work surface around the beaker. If so, your teacher will instruct you how to neutralize it and clean up.

- Measure the mass of the pebble using the laboratory scale. Round the mass to the nearest 0.1 g and record it in the "Mass After" column of the table.

- Calculate how much mass weathered away by subtracting the "after" mass from the "before" mass. Record this number in the "Lost Mass" column.

3. Examine the weathered pebble and write a brief description of its appearance.

_____

_____

_____

- When the other three pebbles have been in the vinegar for 30 minutes, remove them, rinse them off, and dry them with a paper towel.

- Measure the mass of each pebble using the laboratory scale. Round the mass to the nearest 0.1 g and record it in the appropriate row of the "Mass After" column.

- Calculate how much mass weathered away from each pebble by subtracting the "after" mass from the "before" mass. Record these numbers in the appropriate row of the "Lost Mass" column.

4. Did each sample experience chemical weathering? How do you know?

name _____

_____

_____

5. It would be useful to know which kind of weathering is the most effective. However, we can't just look for the biggest loss in mass. Why not?

_____

_____

To know which pebble weathered the most, we must figure out what *percentage* of its mass weathered away. We calculate the percent lost with the following formula:

$$\% \text{ lost} = \frac{\text{Lost Mass (g)}}{\text{Mass Before (g)}} \times 100\%.$$

- Calculate the percentage lost for each row in the table. Round all answers to one decimal place and record them in the "Percent Lost" column.

Sample	Mass Before (g)	Mass After (g)	Lost Mass (g)	Percent Lost
1 (room-temp. vinegar)				
2 (hot vinegar)				
3 (room-temp. vinegar; broken)				
4 (strong acid)				

6. The pebble in the room-temperature vinegar represents normal weathering conditions. The three other pebbles represent single changes we make in the weathering conditions. What kind of experiment have you done? (*Hint*: Review Subsection 1.9 in Chapter 1 of your textbook.)

_____

7. Which type of weathering was the most effective?

_____

8. Which type of weathering was the second-most effective? Explain why.

_____

_____

_____

9. Earlier, we mentioned that some scientists think acids may have formed some kinds of caves. Based on what you've discovered in this lab, why would the acids have had to be stronger and hotter than the kinds involved in normal weathering?

_____

_____

_____

12B Glacier Trek

name _____

section _____   date _____

Unless you live in a mountainous area, you might think of glaciers as something from the Ice Age. But glaciers are very much a part of our modern world. And you really don't have to visit the Alps to see glaciers!

Valley glaciers are still prevalent in parts of the northwestern United States. By studying topographic maps of this region, you can see both their present locations and the results of their past erosional and depositional work. Glaciers and their tributaries appear in white on maps. *Glacial drift*, whether riding on the surface of a glacier or left as a deposit at the sides or end of a glacier, is identified by dotted areas.

Erosional remains of mountains in glaciated areas take the form of *arêtes* or *horns*. Both of these features are identifiable by their closely spaced contour lines: the horns show as single sharp peaks and the arêtes show as elongated narrow ridges. Let's take a virtual glacier trek by studying several maps showing glaciers as well as the consequences of past glacier action.

Procedure

- Examine the map of Mt. Rainier (page 122), a massive composite volcano located in the Cascade Mountains of Washington State.

1. How many named glaciers are there on the flanks of the mountain? Count only those that have the word *Glacier* included in their name.

_____

2. Identify the name and determine to the nearest half kilometer the length of the longest glacier, assuming that it begins at the summit and is continuous.

_____

- The Nisqually Glacier as shown on this map is about 6.4 km long from the summit of the mountain to its terminus. It was observed to retreat a total of 1259 m between 1857 and 1944. Note the moraine that was deposited during the retreat.

3. What map symbol represents moraine material?

_____

- Many of the glaciers exhibit three different levels of gradient (steepness): very steep near the summit, moderately sloping in the middle, and gently sloping near the terminus. Examine Winthrop Glacier.

Goals

After completing this lab, you will be able to

✓ use maps to identify glaciers and measure some of their characteristics.

✓ identify features produced by glacier action.

Equipment

calculator
centimeter ruler
hand magnifier

Mt. Rainier—Dangerous Volcano?

Mt. Rainier's lofty stature and numerous glaciers combine to make it a picturesque sight, visible for many miles in every direction. At present, it is a model of serenity, although some small steam emissions can be seen from time to time, and seismologists have noted a slight increase in the number of minor shallow earthquakes under the volcano. The last recorded eruption occurred in the 1840s. Despite these reassuring statistics, Mt. Rainier is considered one of the most dangerous volcanoes in the world. Due to its huge glaciers, a major eruption could create huge lahars that would sweep down the mountain causing massive destruction in populated areas.

4. How do the map's contour lines indicate the glacier's gradient?

_____

_____

• To determine the gradient from the contour lines, use the map scale to mark a pair of lines 1 km apart on the edge of a small piece of paper.

• Place the paper on the area that you wish to measure. Count the number of contour intervals between the 1 km lines. Remember, the contour intervals are the spaces *in between* the contour lines. Multiply this number by the contour interval value (50 m on this map). The gradient unit is meters per kilometer (m/km).

5. What is the gradient of the Winthrop Glacier near the summit? near the word *Winthrop*? near the word *Glacier*?

_____

• Examine the map of Chugach National Forest in Alaska (page 123). Literally thousands of valley glaciers are contained within the boundaries of this large state, ranging in length from 2–48 km.

6. Judging by the contour lines, in which direction does Heney Glacier move?

_____

• A long, unnamed tributary valley glacier from the west joins Heney Glacier near the northeast corner of the map. The lateral moraines of both glaciers merge.

7. What kind of moraine does this merging form?

_____

8. The margins of the glaciers are marked with small dashed lines. Note that the McCune glacier dies out. It does not reach a lake or river like Heney Glacier. What do you think happens to the ice?

_____

_____

9. A horn appears in map subsection D2. An arête appears in map subsection A25. What is the maximum elevation of each feature? Give your answer in feet.

_____

_____

name_____

- Examine the two maps of southern Wisconsin on page 124. This part of the country is filled with features created by past glacier action. These include *drumlins*, *kettles*, and different kinds of *moraines*. A major difference between this region and the last two regions you studied is that these deposits were caused by a *continental glacier*, not by valley glaciers.

10. Many drumlins appear in the upper map. In what general direction are the drumlins oriented? Express your answer as a hyphenated pair of compass directions.

   _____

11. Based on the orientation of the drumlins, in what direction did the ice sheet move?

   _____

12. Locate Duck Creek to the west of the city of Rome. Study the high drumlin just to the west of the word *Duck*. What is its elevation in feet?

   _____

13. What kind of body of water is in the north side of grid square 31 of the lower map?

   _____

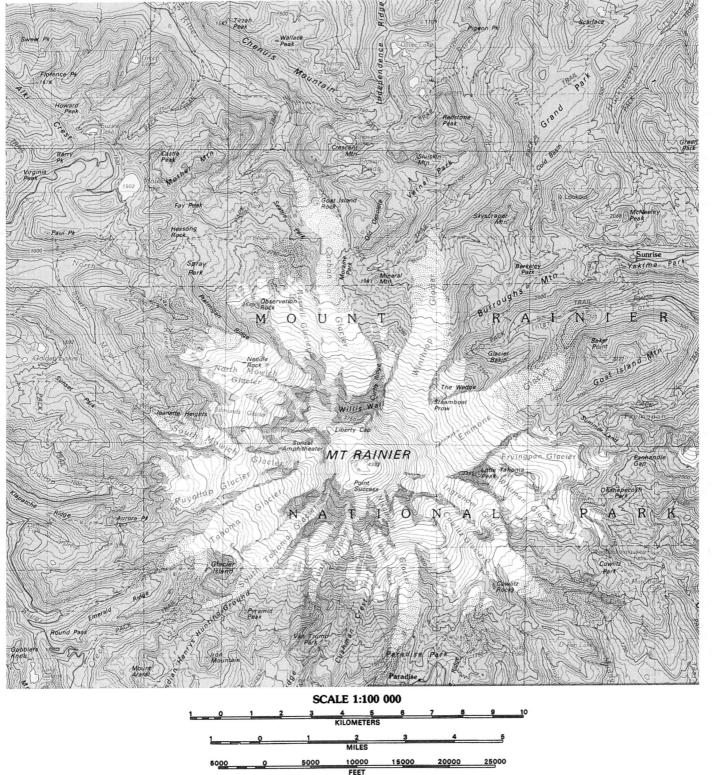

SCALE 1:100 000

KILOMETERS

MILES

FEET

Mt. Rainier Map (Part of the USGS Mt. Rainier Quadrangle, Washington, 1978. Scale 1:100,000; Contour Interval 50 meters)

name ______________________________

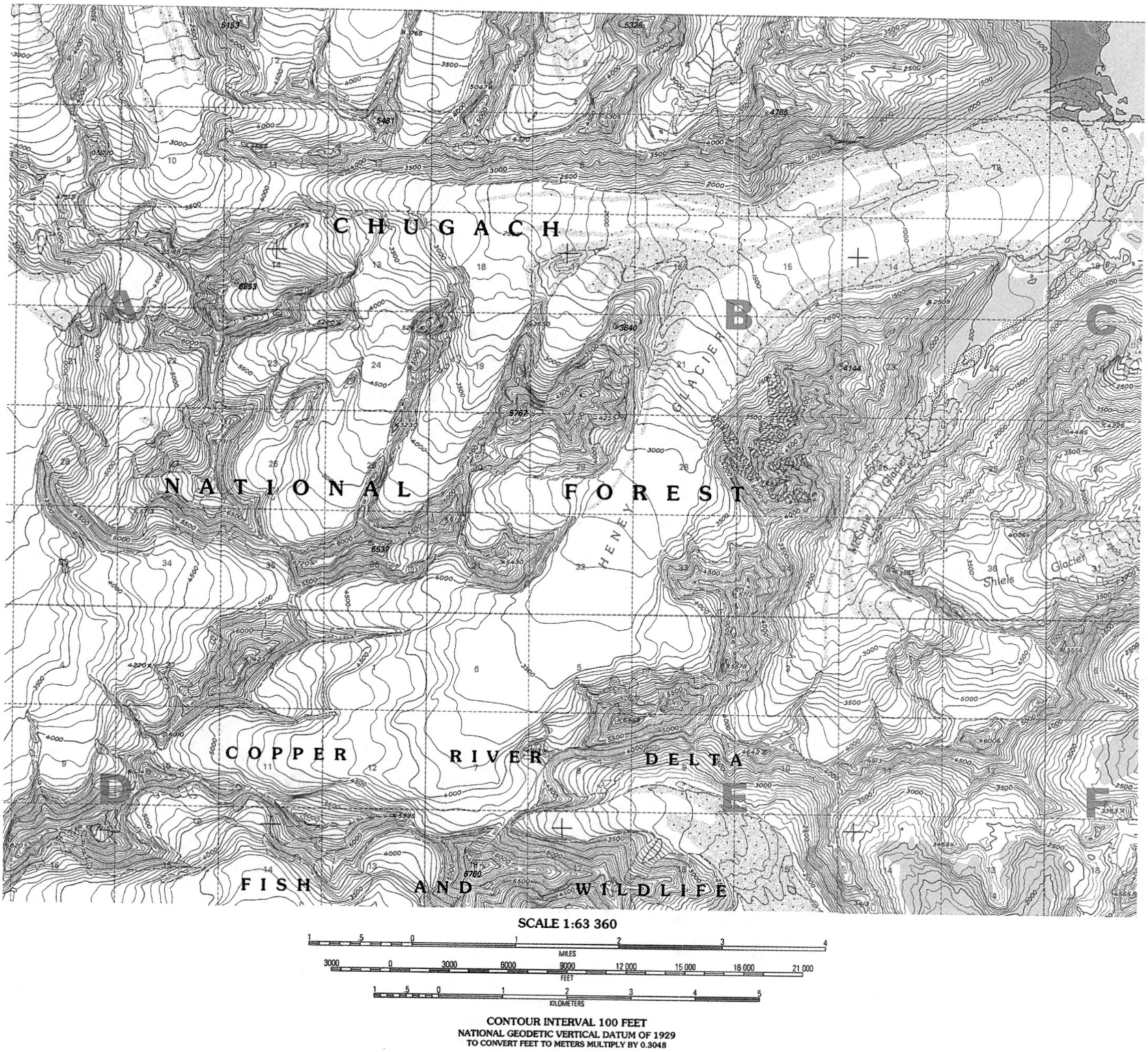

CHUGACH
NATIONAL
FOREST
COPPER
RIVER
DELTA
FISH
AND
WILDLIFE
A
B
C
D
E
F
GLACIER
HENEY
Shiels
Glacier
SCALE 1:63 360
MILES
FEET
KILOMETERS
CONTOUR INTERVAL 100 FEET
NATIONAL GEODETIC VERTICAL DATUM OF 1929
TO CONVERT FEET TO METERS MULTIPLY BY 0.3048

Cordova Map (Part of the USGS Cordova D-3 Quadrangle, Alaska, 1953. Scale 1:63,360; Contour Interval 100 feet)

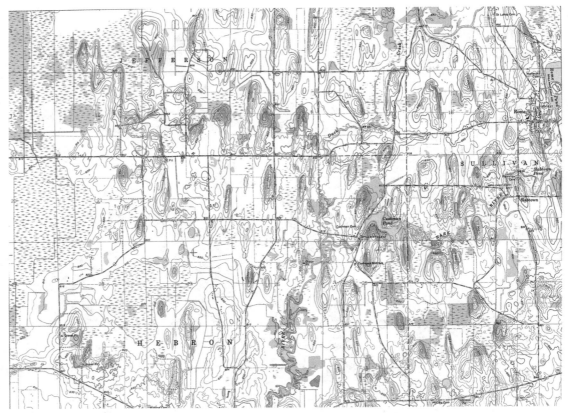

Part of the USGS
Rome Quadrangle,
Wisconsin, 1960/1971.
Scale 1:24,000; Contour
Interval 10 feet

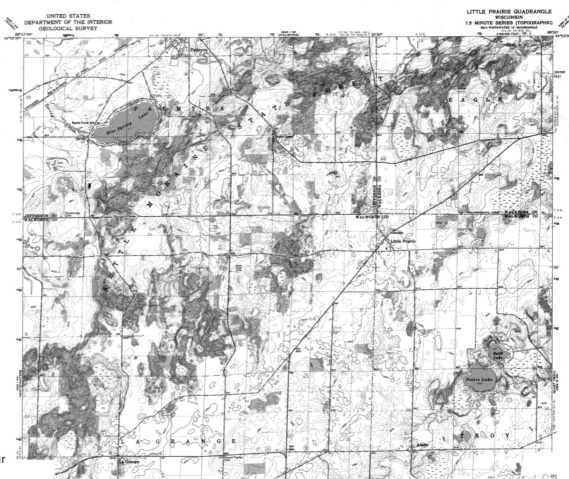

Part of the USGS Little
Prairie Quadrangle,
Wisconsin, 1960/1971.
Scale 1:24,000; Contour
Interval 10 feet

12C Getting Muddy

name_____

section_____ date_____

Most children like to play in the dirt. And some adults never outgrow the habit. They're scientists called *pedologists*, specialists who study soil.

Many people probably think of soil as nothing more than "dirt," a single messy substance. But as you know from your textbook, soil is complicated. In fact, soil contains solids (rocks, sand, silt, clay), liquid (water), gases (air), and organic matter (living and nonliving). It's anything but simple. In this lab, we're going to get muddy as we take apart a soil sample and learn how many different things make up "dirt."

Goals

After completing this lab, you will be able to

✓ identify the various components that make up soil.

✓ measure the components that make up soil.

✓ explain the possible causes for soil variations.

Procedure

- Place a paper towel on the scale. Weigh out 10 g of soil on the paper and take the sample to your desk.

- Spread out the soil sample and use the hand magnifier to examine it carefully.

- Count the live animals (insects, worms, and so forth) that you find and record this number in the table on the next page.

- Mix the sample of soil thoroughly with 250 mL of water in the graduated cylinder.

- Allow the mixture to settle for five minutes. Organic debris should float to the surface, while the rocks and sand will settle to the bottom. Silt and clay remain suspended in the water, making it cloudy.

- While the suspension is settling, place masking tape labels on the three beakers. Label the 1 L beaker "A" and the 250 mL beakers "B" and "C."

- Weigh beakers B and C and record their empty masses in the table.

- Stretch the cheesecloth over the mouth of beaker A. Slowly and carefully pour the cloudy water from the graduated cylinder through the cheesecloth into the beaker. Do *not* pour out the material that settled to the bottom of the graduated cylinder.

- Place the organic debris that got filtered out by the cheesecloth into beaker B.

Equipment

soil sample, 500 g or more
laboratory scale (accurate to 0.1 g)
conventional oven or hot plate
paper towel
centimeter ruler
beaker, 1 L
beakers, 250 mL (2)
graduated cylinder, 250 mL
hand magnifier
cheesecloth
masking tape
hot mitt or pot holder

Figure 1 A typical soil sample can be a lively place!

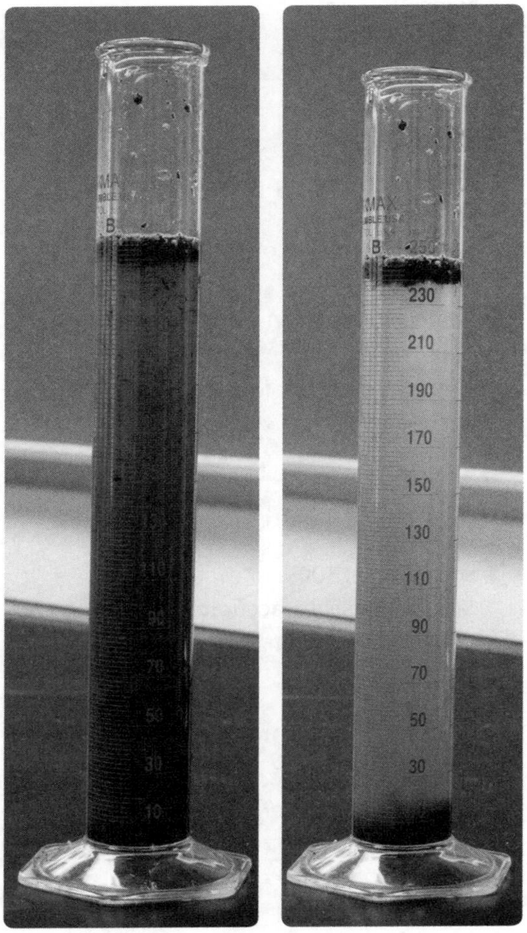

Figure 2 A soil-water mixture settles into its component materials.

- Refill the graduated cylinder with 250 mL of fresh water and thoroughly mix it with the sediment at the bottom. Allow it to settle again. Repeat the previous two steps.
- Repeat the refill/filter cycle until the water is relatively clear after five minutes of settling.
- Transfer the remaining sediment from the graduated cylinder to beaker C. You may need to add a small amount of water to the graduated cylinder to remove all of the sediment. Slowly pour off the excess water from beaker C, being careful not to lose any of the stones or sand.
- Count the number of stones in the wet sediment that are 2–5 mm in diameter and record this number in the table.
- Heat beakers B and C in a 150 °C (300 °F) oven or on a hot plate until their contents are dry (5–20 min). *Be careful not to burn the organic debris.* Using hand protection, remove the beakers and let them cool.
- Weigh beakers B and C and record their full masses in the table. Then, determine the masses of the contents by subtracting the empty beaker masses. Record the final masses in the table.
- Determine the mass of the silt, clay, and water present in the original soil sample by subtracting the masses of the organic debris and the rocks and sand from the starting soil mass of 10 g. Record this value in the table.

Number of Live Animals	Number of Stones	Mass of Silt, Clay, and Water (g)
Masses (g)	**Beaker B (organic debris)**	**Beaker C (rocks and sand)**
Empty		
Full		
Contents		

1. What kinds of materials make up the organic matter found in the soil?

_____

2. What kinds of living organisms did you find in the soil?

_____

_____

_____

name _____

3. What might make the amount of water in different soil samples vary?

_____

_____

_____

4. What might cause the number of living plants and animals in different soil samples to vary?

_____

_____

_____

5. How could the geographic location affect the kind and quantity of rocks and sand found in the sample?

_____

_____

_____

6. How could the depth from which you collect the soil samples affect your results?

_____

_____

_____

7. Why is a thorough understanding of soil composition important for exercising wise dominion over the earth?

_____

_____

_____

_____

13 OCEANS AND SEAS

13A Too Salty?

Is seawater the same wherever you find it? Seawater tastes salty because it contains chemical compounds known as *salts*. We're all familiar with the most common salt, sodium chloride (table salt), but there are many others. When an oceanographer studies the ocean, one of the things he's interested in is the water's saltiness. This is called *salinity*. So, does seawater have the same salinity wherever you find it?

1. Do you think seawater has the same salinity everywhere? Explain why or why not.

_____

_____

_____

What units do we use when we measure salinity? Scientists use several different units, but *parts per thousand* (ppt) is popular. This unit tells you what portion of 1000 parts (by mass) of seawater is salt. For example, if a sample of seawater has a salinity of 35 ppt, the sample is 35 parts salt and 965 parts water.

2. A scientist takes a 500 g sample of water from the Dead Sea and measures its salinity. He finds that it is 326 ppt. In grams, how much of the sample is salt and how much is water?

_____

How do we measure salinity? Scientists use several tools, including *chemical test kits*, *hydrometers*, *refractometers*, and *conductivity meters*. A hydrometer is a weighted glass tube that floats in a sample of seawater. It doesn't measure salinity directly. Instead it measures the *density* of the water. The denser the water, the higher the tube floats. A scale printed on the tube indicates the density.

3. Do you think salt water is denser or less dense than fresh water? Explain why.

_____

_____

_____

We're going to use a hydrometer to measure the salinity of several samples of seawater. Hydrometers report density in *specific gravity* (s.g.) form, which doesn't have units, rather than in the normal density unit of g/cm³.

Goals

After completing this lab, you will be able to
- describe how oceanographers measure salinity.
- measure the salinity of seawater samples.
- create a salinity model of a seawater system.

Equipment

sample containers, 150 mL or larger (5)
graduated cylinder (must fit hydrometer)
hydrometer
thermometer

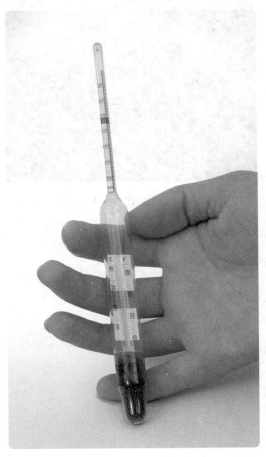

Figure 1 Hydrometers are convenient tools for measuring salinity.

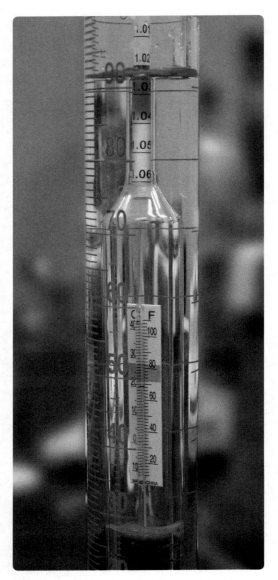

Figure 2 Measuring specific gravity with a hydrometer

Procedure

- If you live near the ocean, collect real seawater. Try to collect it from several different places. A sample from the mouth of a river would be especially useful. Take a sample from a tidal pool. If you have access to a boat, collecting samples from different parts of a bay is also a good idea. Collect enough water to float your hydrometer (at least 150 mL). Keep a record of where you collected each sample.

- If you don't live near the ocean, your teacher will provide you with samples of artificial seawater.

- Fill the graduated cylinder with a seawater sample and carefully float the hydrometer in the water. Tap the cylinder to dislodge any air bubbles from the hydrometer since these will affect the reading. Read the specific gravity by looking at the scale on the hydrometer's side. Record the value in the table on the next page.

- Remove the hydrometer and place the thermometer in the sample. Wait for the thermometer to adjust and record the sample temperature in the table.

- Empty the graduated cylinder. Rinse it and the hydrometer with fresh water.

4. Why is it important to rinse the cylinder and the hydrometer?

_____

_____

- Test each remaining sample and record the data in the table.

- To turn specific gravity into salinity values, you must consult a conversion table or graph and locate your measured specific gravity and temperature. Hydrometers usually come with these tables or graphs, but if yours doesn't, your teacher will provide you with one. Record the salinity in the table.

5. Why do we need to know the sample temperature as well as its specific gravity? (*Hint*: Think about what you learned in Lab 2B.)

_____

_____

_____

name_____

Sample	Specific Gravity	Temperature (°C)	Salinity (ppt)
1			
2			
3			
4			
5			

6. Is salinity the same everywhere?

_____

_____

Optional Activity

If you tested real seawater samples, you can use your data to create a salinity model of the part of the ocean where you collected your water.

- Use an online mapping service to print a map of the area where you collected your samples.

- Mark each location where you collected a sample. Write the salinity next to the mark.

7. Can you draw any conclusions about the relationship of salinity to the location?

_____

_____

_____

13B Low Salt

Is there a lot of water on Earth? Absolutely! The earth contains about 1.3 billion km³ of water. If all of that water were collected into a giant cube, it would be a little over 500 km (311 mi) on a side. However, about 97% of that water is salt water, and most of it is in the oceans. And of the 3% that is fresh, only a fraction of a percent is readily available to us.

Life on land requires fresh water. Industrial processes also require huge amounts of fresh water. If we could figure out how to remove the salt from seawater, our water problems would be over. But taking salt out of seawater, a process called *desalination*, isn't easy. Scientists have discovered several ways to do this. Your textbook mentions two of them: boiling/condensing and reverse osmosis. We're going to take a look at a third method.

To explore desalination, we'll need some artificial seawater. Real seawater contains more than just plain salt (sodium chloride), but salt is the main ingredient. Typical seawater has a salinity of 35 ppt.

1. If you are trying to make up 1000 g of seawater, how much water and how much salt must you mix together? (*Hint*: Water has a mass of 1 g per cm³.)

_____

Procedure

- Use the scale to measure the correct amount of salt. Prepare your artificial seawater by combining the salt and distilled water in the measuring cup and mixing well.

2. Taste the mixture. Is it salty?

_____

One way to remove salt from water is by *freeze desalination*. When water freezes and forms ice crystals, the salt gets forced out because it doesn't fit in the ice's crystal structure.

- Pour about 60 mL of the water into one of the cups. Label the cup "A." Pour the rest of the salt water into the metal mixing bowl and place it in the freezer.

- Monitor the water carefully as it freezes. When the layer of ice is about 3 cm thick, remove the bowl from the freezer. Do *not* allow the water to freeze solid!

- Carefully remove the ice disk from the bowl and place it on the plate. Put it in the freezer for half an hour to solidify so it won't break apart when you handle it.

- Pour about 60 mL of the unfrozen water into the second cup and label it "B."

name_____

section_____   date_____

Goals

After completing this lab, you will be able to
- ✓ prepare artificial seawater.
- ✓ discuss why we desalinate water.
- ✓ compare freeze desalination to other methods of desalination.

Equipment

freezer
measuring cup (1 L or larger)
kitchen scale (accurate to 1 g)
metal mixing bowl
plate
cups (3)
table salt
distilled water

Figure 1 Removing salt from seawater can be quite challenging!

No Tasting!

For safety reasons, we normally never taste things in lab. In this case, however, we are using non-lab equipment that's never been used for other experiments. We're also using food-grade chemicals. So, in this situation it's ok to taste!

Figure 2 Freeze desalination

- Throw away the rest of the unfrozen water and rinse the mixing bowl with fresh water.
- When the ice disk is solidly frozen, rinse it quickly under a stream of cold water, shake it off, and place it in the mixing bowl. Do not rinse it too long or it will melt!
- Wait for the ice disk to melt. Pour about 60 mL of the water from the melted disk into the third cup and label it "C."
- Taste the water in all three cups. Rinse out your mouth with fresh water between tastings.

3. List the cups in increasing order of saltiness.

_____

- Freezing doesn't remove all of the salt. If you wish, you can do another freeze/melt cycle to remove more salt. After several cycles, you will have nearly fresh water.

4. Freeze desalination isn't often used to produce large quantities of fresh water. Do you have any idea why?

_____

_____

Sea ice is ice that forms on the ocean's surface when the seawater gets cold enough to freeze. Icebergs are *not* sea ice. They are chunks of glaciers that have calved and fallen into the water. Icebergs are fresh water.

5. If you were adrift in an open boat and your water had run out, do you think it would be safe to drink melted sea ice? Explain.

_____

_____

6. Why is desalination so important for exercising dominion over the earth?

_____

_____

_____

14 OCEAN MOTIONS

14A Current Events

name _____

section _____   date _____

The ocean is always in motion. Tides, waves, and currents keep its waters flowing. As your textbook explains, there are two types of ocean currents: *surface* and *deep*. Winds drive the surface currents, but their influence doesn't go down very deep. So what moves the deep water?

Although several forces create the deep ocean currents, the most important one is *gravity*. Seawater's density varies considerably due to differences in salinity and temperature. (Remember Labs 13A and 2B?) And as you learned in Lab 5C, gravity pulls denser materials down, forcing up less-dense materials.

In this lab, you're going to build two models of ocean density currents. Each one demonstrates how density keeps the deep ocean in motion.

Goals

After completing this lab, you will be able to
✓ explain how salinity affects deep ocean currents.
✓ demonstrate how density differences create layers in the ocean.

Equipment

2× cold seawater, 100 mL
2× room-temperature seawater, 25 mL
blue and yellow food coloring
long-stemmed funnel
wide-mouthed jars, 1 L (2)
beaker, 50 mL
small glass square or watch glass
white paper

Procedure

• Look at Figure 14-20 in your textbook. It shows how seawater with different densities flows between the Mediterranean Sea and the Atlantic Ocean.

1. What is the major cause of the density differences in this water?

   _____

• Look at Figure 14-19 in your textbook. It shows the major deep ocean currents. The most significant of these is the *thermohaline circulation*.

2. What causes the density differences in the water that makes up the thermohaline circulation?

   _____

   _____

• Fill one of the jars with 500 mL of room-temperature fresh water.

• Place the 50 mL beaker inside the jar. Place the glass plate or watch glass on top of the beaker. If you use a watch glass, the curved side should face down. The plate models an underwater ledge.

• Add a few drops of blue food coloring to 25 mL of the room-temperature 2× seawater so it turns a deep inky color.

3. Which water is denser, the fresh water or the 2× seawater? Explain why.

   _____

   _____

2×?

You may be wondering what we mean by 2× seawater. The 2× refers to the water's salinity compared to "normal" seawater (35 ppt). The 2× seawater contains twice as much salt as normal seawater, so it's much more saline (70 ppt).

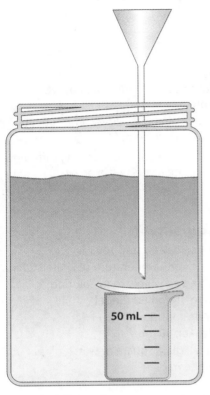

Figure 1 Modeling a deep ocean current

Don't Exaggerate?

You may wonder why we're using fresh water and 2× seawater to model the ocean. The reason is that we have to exaggerate the effect that happens in the real ocean in order to see it in our model. Actual seawater density differences are usually smaller than those in our model. Our model is much smaller than the real ocean, so we wouldn't be able to see the effects of density if we used more "realistic" water.

Don't think of model exaggeration as dishonest, however! Scientists use this method all the time to make effects easier to see. Remember how you exaggerated the volcano profile in Lab 8B so you could get a better impression of the mountain's contours?

Engineers often use "exaggerated" techniques for testing their designs. Life testing an engine would take years if it were done normally! So engineers deliberately exaggerate operating conditions to make the engine wear out rapidly. This kind of testing is called *accelerated testing*.

- Hold the funnel in the jar so that the end of the stem is just above the glass plate. You're going to use it to pour the seawater into the fresh water without causing a lot of commotion.
- Place a sheet of white paper behind the jar to make the colors stand out more clearly.

4. Describe what you think will happen when you add the seawater to the fresh water. Be sure to explain the reasons behind what you expect to happen.

_____

_____

_____

- Slowly and gently, pour the 2× seawater into the funnel. Observe what happens as it lands on the glass plate.

5. Did the seawater behave as you predicted? Explain.

_____

_____

- Fill the second jar with 500 mL of the hottest water you can get from the faucet.
- Add *one* drop of yellow food coloring to the hot water. Add a few drops of blue food coloring to 100 mL of the cold 2× seawater.
- Hold the funnel in the jar so that the end of the stem is near the bottom. You're going to use it to pour the seawater into the fresh water without causing a lot of commotion.
- Place a sheet of white paper behind the jar to make the colors stand out more clearly.

6. Describe what you think will happen when you add the cold 2× seawater to the fresh hot water. Be sure to explain the reasons behind what you expect to happen.

_____

_____

_____

- Slowly and gently, pour the 2× seawater into the funnel. Observe what happens.

7. Did the water behave as you predicted? Explain.

_____

_____

8. Match textbook Figures 14-19 and 14-20 with the jar that best models the current the figure illustrates.

name _____

_____

_____

9. What do you think will happen if you let the second jar sit undisturbed for ten minutes? How will you be able to tell if your prediction is correct?

_____

_____

_____

- Let the second jar sit for ten minutes without being disturbed. Observe what happens.

10. Did the water behave as you predicted? Explain.

_____

_____

14B Making Waves

name_____

section_____   date_____

As you learned in Chapter 1, a tsunami can be a frightening and fatal event. These giant waves rush ashore with little warning, destroying everything in their path. But as you also learned from the story of Tilly Smith, little warning is not the same as none. Tilly remembered what she had learned in school. So she was able to spot the signs of an approaching tsunami and warn those around her just minutes before it arrived.

A tsunami begins in the deep ocean when a seismic event puts a lot of energy into the water and starts a wave moving outward. What does the wave look like out in the ocean? And how does it turn into a giant wall of water when it comes ashore? We're going to get some answers by modeling a tsunami's speed and wave height as it moves from open ocean toward the shore.

Procedure

- Scientists have discovered that a tsunami's speed partly depends upon how much water is below it. The following formula gives the wave's speed (in km/h) for a given ocean depth:

$$\text{wave speed} = \sqrt{127 \times \text{depth (m)}}.$$

- Calculate the wave speed for each depth shown in the table on the next page. Round the speeds to the nearest km/h and record them in the table.

- Using the first graphing area on page 142, create a graph that models wave speed compared to the ocean's depth. The x-axis is the depth. The y-axis is the wave speed. Draw a smooth curve through the points.

1. Does a tsunami travel quickly or slowly in deep water? What about in shallow water?

_____

_____

2. The Indian Ocean Tsunami of 2004 destroyed villages in the African country of Somalia, 4500 km away from the tsunami's point of origin. It took seven hours to reach Somalia. Assuming a constant speed, how fast was the tsunami traveling in km/h?

_____

Goals

After completing this lab, you will be able to

✓ graph a tsunami's speed at different ocean depths.

✓ graph a tsunami's wave height at different ocean depths.

✓ explain how depth affects a tsunami's behavior.

Equipment

graph paper (included)
calculator

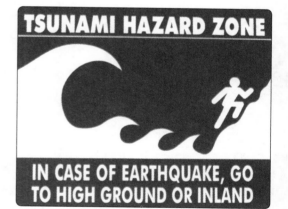

Figure 1 Being alert to the dangers of tsunamis can save lives!

As you can see from your calculations, a tsunami's speed changes with depth. However, the wave's *energy* doesn't change. If the wave's speed changes, something else must also change or the energy won't stay the same.

3. What scientific principle says that energy can be changed but cannot be created or destroyed? (*Hint*: Review Subsection 2.11 in Chapter 2.)

_____

_____

_____

- As a tsunami's speed changes with depth, its height will change so it doesn't violate this scientific principle. The following formula can be used to estimate the tsunami's height (in meters) for a given depth (in meters):

$$\text{wave height} = \sqrt{\sqrt{\frac{2000}{\text{depth (m)}}}}.$$

- Calculate the wave height for each depth shown in the table. Round the heights to one decimal place and record them in the table.

- Using the second graphing area on page 142, create a graph that models wave height compared to the ocean's depth. The *x*-axis is the depth. The *y*-axis is the wave height. Draw a smooth curve through the points.

Depth (m)	Speed (km/h)	Height (m)
1000		
800		
600		
400		
200		
100		
80		
60		
40		
20		
10		

Seeing Double?

Don't be alarmed by the double square root in the formula! It simply means that you should hit your calculator's square root button twice in a row. For example, to calculate the wave height at a depth of 200 m, key in

$$2000 \div 200 = \sqrt{}\ \sqrt{}.$$

4. What happens to the tsunami's height as it moves from deep to shallow water?

name_____

_____

_____

5. Do you think a ship out in deep ocean would notice a tsunami? Why or why not?

_____

_____

6. Based upon what you've learned, explain why people living on the shore often don't realize that a tsunami is coming until it's too late to escape.

_____

_____

_____

7. Why is a tsunami's great speed out at sea another reason that people don't know they are in danger until the wave arrives?

_____

_____

_____

8. In a few sentences describe how a tsunami forms, how it travels, and how it behaves when it comes to land.

_____

_____

_____

_____

9. Why would constructing a tsunami early warning system be an example of good dominion and loving one's neighbor?

_____

_____

_____

Wave Speed vs. Depth

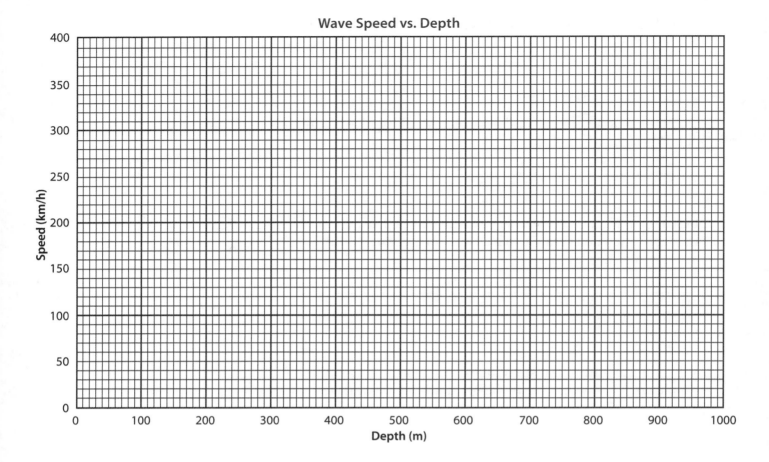

Wave Height vs. Depth

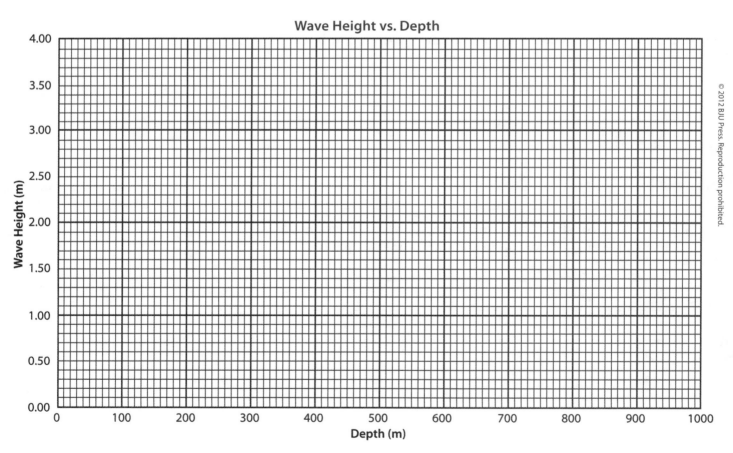

15 OCEAN EXPLORATION

15A Taking a Bath

name _____

section _____ date _____

Remember Google Earth™? We said that Google Earth™ "will be your virtual airplane and submarine as you explore earth science this year." You've already used it as an airplane. Now it's time to use it to dive beneath the ocean depths!

Oceanographers map the features of the ocean floor using a technique called *bathymetry*. This simply means "deep measuring." In the early days of oceanography, scientists measured the ocean depths by dropping a weighted rope called a *lead line* (pronounced like the metal) over the ship's side to the bottom. Later, they used sonar to produce more detailed pictures. Today, oceanographers use very sophisticated sonar systems, LIDAR, and satellites to create very detailed pictures of the ocean bottom.

Much of this data has been built into Google Earth™, making it easy to explore the many interesting features of the ocean floor. In this lab, you're going to use bathymetric data to explore the ocean bottom just like a research submarine does. And you'll never even have to leave your desk!

Procedure

- Start Google Earth™. Uncheck all of the checkboxes under the **Layers** list except for **Border and Labels**.

- Select the **View** menu and make sure **Water Surface** is checked.

- Select the **Tools** menu. Select **Options**. Select the **3D View** tab. Be sure **Units of Measurement** is set to **Meters, Kilometers**. Also, check the **Show terrain** box and slide the **Terrain Quality** slider all the way to the right. Click **OK**.

- Find the state of Rhode Island and zoom in so your **Eye alt** is between 400–450 km.

- Look straight south. You'll notice that the ocean is light blue near land and dark blue farther south. Color in Google Earth™ indicates depth. The darker the blue, the deeper the ocean.

- You can find the ocean depth at any point by moving your mouse pointer over the area of interest. Look at the bottom center of the screen near the word **elev**. The number after it indicates your elevation. If the number is negative, the reference is to the ocean's depth at that point. Move your mouse pointer just south of Block Island.

Goals

After completing this lab, you will be able to

✓ use Google Earth™ to examine the ocean floor.

✓ create an underwater profile.

✓ identify and explore underwater features.

Equipment

computer with Google Earth™

Bouncing Around

All of the modern bathymetry tools mentioned here rely on echoes to measure the ocean floor. Sonar works by bouncing sound waves off the ocean bottom and measuring the time it takes for the echo to come back. LIDAR does the same thing, but uses a laser beam instead of sound. Satellites bounce radio waves (radar) off the ocean's *surface*, to detect what lies beneath.

sonar: **so**und **na**vigation and **r**anging

LIDAR: **li**ght **d**etection **a**nd **r**anging

radar: **ra**dio **d**etection **a**nd **r**anging

© 2011 Europa Technologies/©2011 Google/Data SIO, NOAA, U.S. Navy, NGA, GEBCO

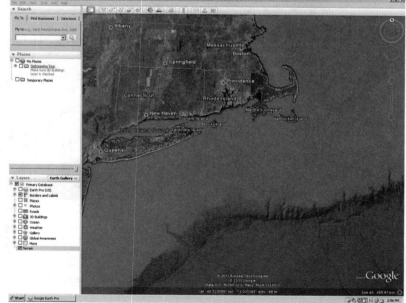

Figure 1

1. What is the ocean depth at this point?

_____

• Keep moving south until you reach the edge of the light blue part of the sea floor. Note the depth as you move along.

2. What is the range of depth from Block Island to the edge of the light blue area?

_____

3. Based upon what you've learned, what is this part of the ocean floor called? (*Hint*: Review Figure 13-7 in your textbook.)

_____

• Keep moving south. You'll notice a band of darker ocean floor. Watch the depth as you move through this band.

4. Does the depth change slowly or quickly?

_____

5. What is this area of the ocean floor called?

_____

• Move farther south out of the band and into the dark blue ocean. Watch the depth as you move around this area.

6. Does the ocean floor keep going downward?

_____

7. What is this area of the ocean floor called?

_____

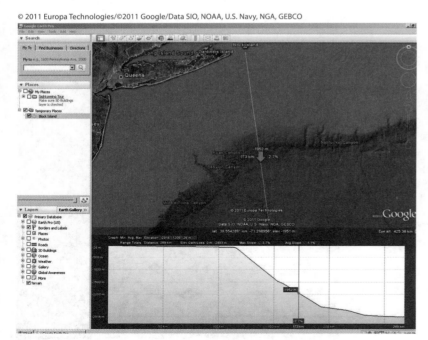

Figure 2

It's not very easy to get a feel for the ocean bottom just by looking at numbers. Let's build a *profile* of the ocean floor, similar to the ones we created for mountains in Labs 7B and 8B. In fact, Google Earth™ can do this task automatically.

• Check the **Temporary Places** checkbox in the **Places** list.

• Click the **Add Path** button in the toolbar at the top of the screen. Position the mouse pointer just south of Block Island and click the left button. Position the mouse pointer near the head of the Hudson Valley (SSE of Block Island) and click the left button. A line, called a *path*, should appear between the two points.

name_____

- Click the **Altitude** tab in the **New Path** dialog box. Change **Altitude** to **Clamped to sea floor**. Change the **Name** from **Untitled Path** to **Block Island**. Click **OK**.

- Find your new **Block Island** path under **Temporary Places**. Right-click it. Pick **Show Elevation Profile** from the pop-up menu that appears. Google Earth™ will build a profile of the ocean floor along the path from Block Island to Hudson Valley.

- Examine the profile. It's exaggerated to make the contours easy to see. The true profile is less dramatic. If you place the mouse anywhere inside the profile and slide it left or right, a vertical line will appear on top of the profile. The ocean depth is the number at the top of the line. The distance along the path is the number at the bottom.

8. How far south of Block Island does the continental shelf end?

_____

9. How far south along the path does the continental slope end?

_____

10. How deep does the abyssal plain get within the profile?

_____

- Let's examine an underwater valley. Close the profile by clicking the ☒ in its upper-right corner. Move your position so that the south end of the path is in the middle of the screen. Adjust your **Eye alt** to about 40 km.

- Click the mouse wheel and pull the mouse toward you. The view will tilt until you suddenly go underwater. Congratulations! You're a submarine.

- Adjust the tilt until you can see the Hudson Valley easily. You can explore the valley by clicking the left mouse button and dragging back and forth. Spend a few moments moving along the length of the valley.

- Uncheck the **Borders and Labels** checkbox under **Layers**.

- **Fly to** the following location: **37.416N 70.871W**

- Adjust your **Eye alt** to 2–3 km.

- Click the mouse wheel and pull the mouse toward you. The view will tilt until you are under water and the feature of interest will become visible.

> ### Keyboard Reminder
> If you don't have a mouse with a wheel, you can tilt the perspective by holding down the **Shift** key and using the **Up** and **Down** arrow keys.

© 2011 Europa Technologies/©2011 Google/Image USDA Farm Service Agency/ Data SIO, NOAA, U.S. Navy, NGA, GEBCO

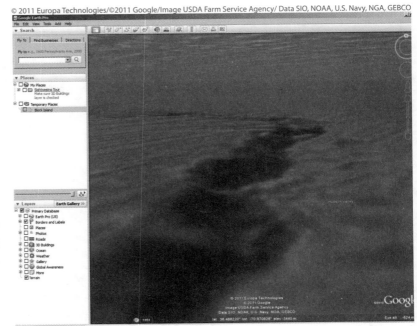

Figure 3

11. What are you looking at?

_____

12. What's the sea bottom like around this feature?

_____

_____

- There are many more of these features southeast of Nova Scotia. Spend a few minutes exploring them. If you check the **Border and Labels** checkbox, their names will appear.

Optional Activity

- Re-create the historic descent into the Challenger Deep made by *Trieste* in 1960. Locate the Challenger Deep and visit it with Google Earth.™ Make a profile of the ocean floor. (*Hint*: See textbook pages 303 and 364–65.)

15B Dive, Dive!

name_____

section_____   date_____

Submarines help an oceanographer to "be there" when he studies the ocean. For centuries, scientists wished to travel underwater so they could study the seas up close. But until the twentieth century, submarines were primitive and dangerous. Submarines contain many different technologies, which is the reason they took so long to perfect.

One technology that all submarines need is a reliable system to make the boat submerge and surface. Being able to control a submarine's position in the water can be a matter of life or death. What makes a submarine sink and rise in the water? Buoyancy! An object's *buoyancy* is its tendency to sink or float. Buoyancy depends upon two things: the object's *volume* and its *mass*. Let's explore the role that these two properties play in an object's buoyancy.

Procedure

- Take a look at the pill bottle. Imagine pushing it into a container of water until it's completely submerged.

1. What happens to the water when you push the bottle under the surface?

_____

We call this behavior *displacement*. But can we know how much water an object displaces? Absolutely! An object's displacement equals its volume. Imagine a hole in the water shaped just like the pill bottle. If we could pour the water that would fill up that hole into a graduated cylinder, we would know the object's displacement. Let's measure the pill bottle's displacement.

- Fill the bottle with sand and snap on the cap. Cut a 50 cm length of thread and tie a loop around the bottle below the cap.

- Fill the graduated cylinder about half full. Record the volume of water in the graduated cylinder rounded to the nearest division on the cylinder.

_____

- Slowly lower the bottle into the graduated cylinder until it's completely submerged.

2. Explain what happens to the water in the cylinder.

_____

Goals

After completing this lab, you will be able to
- ✓ explain why objects float or sink.
- ✓ measure an object's displacement.
- ✓ calculate the ballast needed to make an object hover in water.
- ✓ apply what you've learned to submarines.

Equipment

pill bottle with cap
laboratory scale (accurate to 0.1 g)
beaker, 1 L
graduated cylinder, 500 mL
fine sand
salt
strong thread

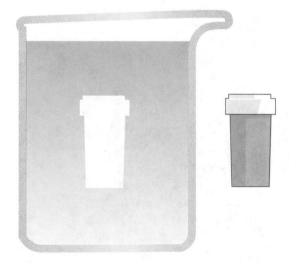

Figure 1 Displacement

Figure 2 Measuring the bottle's displacement

Staying Neutral

An object that hovers in the water is said to be *neutrally buoyant*. Objects that sink are *negatively buoyant*, while those that float are *positively buoyant*.

Figure 3 Almost (but not quite) neutrally buoyant

- Record the volume of water in the graduated cylinder rounded to the nearest division on the cylinder.

_____

3. What must you do to determine the pill bottle's volume?

_____

_____

- Calculate and record the pill bottle's volume in cm³. (*Hint*: 1 cm³ = 1 mL.)

_____

- Remove the pill bottle, dry it off, and empty the sand. Weigh the empty bottle and cap. Record the mass rounded to the nearest 0.1 g.

_____

What determines whether an object sinks or floats? An object floats if the mass of the water it displaces is greater than the object's mass. It sinks if the mass of the water it displaces is less than the object's mass. If the two masses are equal, the object "hovers" in the water, neither rising nor sinking.

4. If you want the pill bottle to hover in the water, how much mass must you add to it? (*Hint*: 1 cm³ of water has a mass of 1 g.)

_____

- Using the laboratory scale, weigh the amount of sand equal to the calculated mass. Pour the sand into the bottle.
- Fill the beaker with 1 L of water. Cap the bottle and carefully lower it into the beaker. It should hover, neither rising nor sinking. You may have to "tweak" the amount of sand to get it perfectly balanced.

5. How does what you have observed with the pill bottle apply to submarines?

_____

_____

6. The pill bottle floated or sank depending upon its displacement (volume) and its mass. What physical property have you already studied that is based on these two quantities?

_____

7. What happens to this property of the pill bottle when you change its mass?

_____

8. What do you think will happen to your perfectly balanced bottle if you place it in salt water instead of fresh? (*Hint*: Is salt water denser or less dense than fresh water?)

_____

• Test your hypothesis by adding 36 g of salt to the water in the 1 L beaker and stirring well. Slowly lower the bottle into the salt water.

9. What happens to the bottle when you place it in salt water?

_____

10. What must you do to make the bottle hover instead of float?

_____

As you learned in Labs 13A and 14A, seawater's density varies from place to place. Submarines must be able to adjust to the differing densities of the local water to control their vertical position.

11. Explain one way that submarines can adjust their position in the water.

_____

_____

_____

name_____

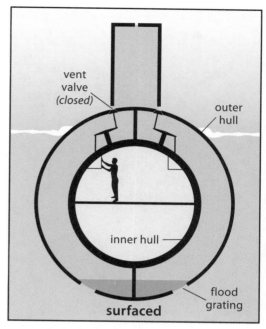

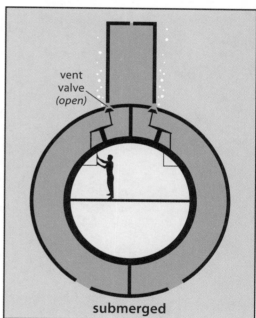

Figure 4 Submarines use ballast tanks to change their density.

16 SURFACE WATERS

16A Surface Impressions

Earth has some fascinating bodies of water. Not only are some of them amazingly beautiful, but some are also incredibly strange. Visiting these bodies of water would take a lot of time and money. But thanks to GIS tools like Google Earth™, you can visit them easily. Even more importantly, thanks to some of the tools built into the program, you can visit them as a scientist rather than as just a tourist.

In this lab, we're going to examine several lakes and one river. All three lakes are pretty unusual in some special way. And while the river is not particularly unusual, you're going to use it to test some of the concepts found in your textbook.

Procedure 1 (A Crater Lake)

- Start Google Earth™. Uncheck all of the checkboxes under the **Layers** list except for **Border and Labels**.

- Select the **Tools** menu. Select **Options**. Select the **3D View** tab. Be sure **Units of Measurement** is set to **Meters, Kilometers**. Also, confirm that **Show terrain** is checked and the **Terrain Quality** slider is all the way to the right. Click **OK**.

- **Fly to** the following location: **Crater Lake, OR**. Adjust your **Eye alt** to 12–15 km.

Crater Lake, as its name implies, is a lake formed in the caldera of Mt. Mazama, a collapsed volcano. It's a typical example of this type of lake.

1. What is the elevation of the north side of the lake? What about the south side? What is the elevation of the lake surface?

  _____

  _____

  _____

- Zoom in on Wizard Island and examine it closely.

2. What do you think Wizard Island is?

  _____

- Zoom back out to an **Eye alt** of 12–15 km. Let's build a profile of the surrounding mountain and lake surface. It will give us a "side view" of the lake.

- Check the **Temporary Places** checkbox in the **Places** list.

- Click the **Add Path** button in the toolbar at the top of the screen. Position the mouse pointer above the north rim of the lake and click the left button. Position the mouse pointer below the south rim of the lake and click the left button. A line, called a *path*, should appear between the two points.

© 2012 BJU Press. Reproduction prohibited.

name _____

section _____ date _____

Special Lake

Tourists and scientists consider Crater Lake unusual for several reasons. Its dark blue waters are amazingly clear and beautiful. Secchi disks can be seen from as deep as 20–30 m! It is also the deepest lake in the United States (594 m) as well as the second-deepest lake in North America.

Figure 1 Wizard Island

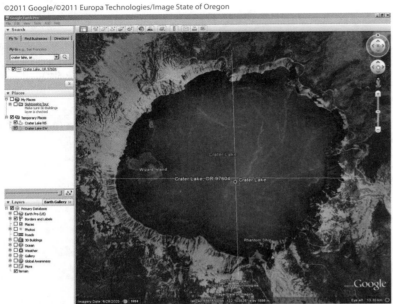

©2011 Google/©2011 Europa Technologies/Image State of Oregon

Figure 2

- Click the **Altitude** tab in the **New Path** dialog box. Make sure **Altitude** is **Clamped to ground**. Change the **Name** from **Untitled Path** to **Crater Lake NS**. Click **OK**.

- Add a second path that runs from the left of the west rim of the lake, through the center of Wizard Island, to the right of the east rim of the lake. Make its name **Crater Lake EW**.

- Find the **Crater Lake NS** path under **Temporary Places**. Right-click it. Pick **Show Elevation Profile** from the pop-up menu that appears. Google Earth™ will build a profile of the lake rim and surface along the N-S path.

3. Is the lake a uniformly deep basin from north to south? In other words, are the north and south rims about the same elevation?

_____

- Find the **Crater Lake EW** path under **Temporary Places**. Right-click it. Pick **Show Elevation Profile** from the pop-up menu that appears. Google Earth™ will build a profile of the lake rim and surface along the E-W path.

4. Is the lake a uniformly deep basin from east to west?

_____

5. How high is the summit of Wizard Island above the lake's surface? (*Hint*: The bottom of the profile represents the water's surface.)

_____

- Close the profile by clicking the ⊠ in its upper-right corner. Adjust your position so the lake is in the center of the screen. Your **Eye alt** should still be 12–15 km.

- Click the mouse wheel and pull the mouse toward you. The view will tilt, looking more and more like a real landscape. Adjust the tilt so the earth looks almost flat. Spend a few moments exploring the caldera basin, Wizard Island, and the surrounding landscape.

Procedure 2 (Low Lakes)

- **Fly to** the coordinates **32.173N 35.560E**. Adjust your **Eye alt** to 200–250 km and move this position to the center of the screen.

You're looking at the State of Israel with the Sea of Galilee at the top and the Dead Sea at the bottom. Both of these lakes are unusual bodies of water! The Jordan River connects them. It, by contrast, is just an ordinary stream.

Doubly Special

The Sea of Galilee has the distinction of being the lowest *freshwater* lake in the world. The Dead Sea is the lowest *saltwater* lake in the world. It is also the lowest dry land location on Earth! Both bodies of water appear frequently in the Bible.

- Zoom in on the Sea of Galilee to an **Eye alt** of about 20–25 km.

1. What is the elevation at the center of the Sea of Galilee?

name_____

_____

- Move south until you have the Dead Sea centered on the screen. Keep the **Eye alt** the same.

2. What is the elevation at the center of the Dead Sea?

_____

- Zoom back out. Using the **Ruler** tool, measure the distance in meters between the southern end of the Sea of Galilee and the northern end of the Dead Sea. Round the number to the nearest 1000 m and record it below.

_____

As your textbook explains, a stream's *gradient* is the steepness of its slope. Large gradient values indicate a steep slope. To calculate the gradient, we divide the stream's drop in elevation from one end to the other by the length of the stream. Gradient is expressed as a percent. The following formula lets you calculate the gradient:

Figure 3 The Dead Sea's high salinity has some unusual effects!

$$\text{Gradient} = \frac{\text{High Elevation (m)} - \text{Low Elevation (m)}}{\text{Length of Stream (m)}} \times 100\%.$$

- Calculate the Jordan River's gradient. Both elevations should be expressed as negative numbers. Round your answer to one decimal place and record it below.

_____

- Review the stream features discussed on pages 377–79 of your textbook.

3. Based on the Jordan River's gradient and what you've learned from the textbook, what do you expect the Jordan River to do as it flows south? Explain why.

_____

_____

- Let's see if the Jordan River follows your predictions. Zoom in on the Jordan River somewhere in between the two lakes. Adjust your **Eye alt** to about 2–3 km.

4. What does the Jordan River do as it flows south? Does it do what you predicted in question 3?

_____

_____

Ancient Propaganda?

Naaman's scornful opinion of the Jordan River appears in 2 Kings 5:12. As an extra activity, you may want to use Google Earth™ to compare the Jordan to the Abana River that Naaman was so proud of. It's the modern Barada River in Syria. **Fly to** the coordinates **33.515N 36.312E** and measure the river's width with the **Ruler** tool. It's possible that Naaman's boast was nothing more than ancient propaganda!

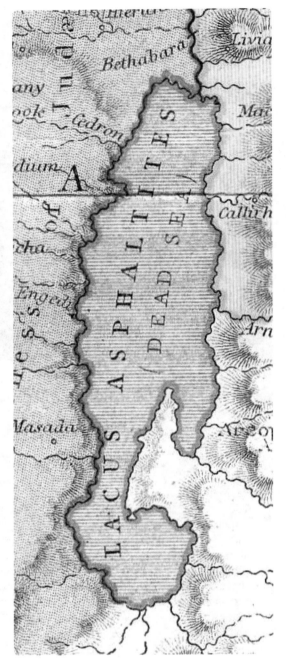

Figure 4 The Dead Sea has changed since this map was made.

- Zoom in on the Dead Sea so it fills the screen. Notice that it is actually *two* bodies of water separated by a narrow strip of land. A peninsula projects into the upper body of the lake from the southern end.
- Examine the lower body of water. It's crisscrossed by lines. These are part of a huge industrial salt extraction facility that's in this part of the lake.

Until a few decades ago, the Dead Sea was one single body of water. The peninsula that you see today used to be a large boot-shaped spit of land called the Lisan Peninsula that entered the lake from its eastern shore.

Over time, agriculture and industry drained water from the Jordan River. The Dead Sea began to shrink until the peninsula divided the lake into two separate parts. If you examine maps of Israel such as those found in older Bibles, you can compare the Dead Sea of the recent and ancient past to its current state today.

In 2009, the Jordan Red Sea Project (JRSP) company proposed a plan that would help restore the Dead Sea to its former level. More importantly, it would also provide large quantities of fresh water to the nearby Kingdom of Jordan. The plan is to take salt water from the Gulf of Aqaba on the Red Sea and pipe it into Jordan where it will be desalinated. The fresh water will be used by people and industry in Jordan. Meanwhile, the brine produced by the desalination process will drain into the Dead Sea, raising its level.

5. Briefly discuss how projects like the JRSP are examples of good dominion.

_____

_____

_____

Optional Activity

- Build a profile from the north of the Sea of Galilee to the south of the Dead Sea. Follow the Jordan River very closely as you move south.
- Use the same procedure that you used to profile Crater Lake. Since the Jordan River isn't straight, you will need to create a path made up of many short line segments that follow the river's bends and loops.
- To follow the river closely, zoom in to an **Eye alt** of about 25 km. You will need to hit the **Down** arrow key on your keyboard every time you get to the bottom of the screen so you can keep moving south to the Dead Sea. The more carefully you create the path, the better the final profile will look.

16B Being *Too* Green?

Is it possible to be too "green"? If you've ever seen a lake that looked like pea soup, you know the answer is *yes*. When you see water thick with algae, you're seeing *eutrophication* at work. Eutrophication (Gk. *eutrophia*—well nourished) is a condition in which bodies of water contain too many nutrients. Explosions of algae, called *algal blooms*, occur, making the water murky and unpleasant. When the algae die, they sink to the bottom and start to decay. Water oxygen levels drop, and other plants and animals can die.

Water plants need *nitrogen* and *phosphorus* to live and grow. But too much of either causes problems. Excessive nutrients can come from many places. Runoff from fertilized fields, sewage, industrial waste, and some detergents can lead to eutrophication. Many states have banned phosphates from household detergents to reduce algal blooms.

In this lab, we're going to explore nutrient levels in local water systems. We'll use two simple test kits to measure the nitrogen and phosphorus levels in water samples. Scientists, aquarium hobbyists, and industrial technicians use kits like these to check water chemistry quickly and easily.

name_____

section_____   date_____

Goals

After completing this lab, you will be able to

✓ explain the causes and consequences of eutrophication.

✓ use a water chemistry test kit.

✓ test local water for eutrophication conditions.

Equipment

nitrate test kit
phosphate test kit
sample containers, 100 mL (5)
distilled water

Procedure

- Collect five water samples from local rivers, streams, lakes, or ponds. If you can find a lake or pond showing an algal bloom, try to find the water source that feeds the body. Collect a sample from this place rather than from the body itself. You may also want to collect multiple samples from different parts of a large body of water.

- Rinse the container in the water you're sampling before you capture the actual sample. Cap and label the container.

- Look around you and make a few notes about the surrounding environment. Pay special attention to farmlands, factories, bright green (fertilized) lawns and gardens, as well as other potential sources of runoff.

- Test the samples for nitrate and phosphate levels. Carefully follow the directions that come with your test kit. In most cases, you will fill a test tube with a specific volume of water and add a specific number of drops of a test solution. After waiting for several minutes, you then compare the sample's color to a color reference card. The color indicates the water's nitrate or phosphate level. If possible, view the colors in natural daylight.

- Between tests, rinse the test tube very thoroughly so the previous test doesn't contaminate the next one. If you have several test tubes, perform all of the tests at the same time.

Figure 1 "Red tides" are one kind of algal bloom.

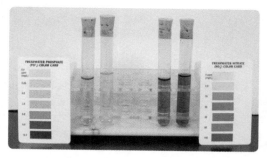

Figure 2 Testing water samples for nitrate and phosphate levels

- After you've tested your water samples, do two more tests, one with distilled water and one with tap water. If you have access to an aquarium, test a sample of its water as well. Record all test results as well as the sample source place names in the table below.

Sample	Nitrate (ppm)	Phosphate (ppm)
distilled water		
tap water		
aquarium water		

1. Which sample showed the highest nitrate and/or phosphate level?

   _____

2. Why do you think it had these levels?

   _____

   _____

3. Did the distilled water and tap water samples contain nitrate and/or phosphate? Explain why or why not.

   _____

   _____

   _____

4. Were you able to observe signs of eutrophication? If so, did your test results support the idea that high nutrient levels are behind these signs? Explain.

   _____

   _____

   _____

5. Why is preventing eutrophication a good example of exercising wise dominion?

name_____

_____

_____

_____

6. Should humans stop fertilizing fields to prevent algal blooms in nearby water sources? Explain.

_____

_____

_____

_____

_____

17 GROUNDWATER

17A Perking *Down*

name_____

section_____ date_____

When you drink a glass of cold water on a hot day, do you ever stop to think about where it comes from? It often comes from the *groundwater system*. Think of the groundwater system as a series of giant storage tanks buried in the ground. They capture rainwater and store it until we're ready to use it. Wells and springs bring it to the surface, and from there it's just a short trip to your glass.

The groundwater storage tanks aren't made of metal though! They're made up of layers of rock, sand, clay, and other natural materials. Water collects inside or gets trapped between these layers. How the system works depends upon the materials the layers are made of.

In this lab, we're going to model the groundwater system. We'll see how rainwater enters the ground and passes through some of the system's layers. Other layers stop the water or absorb it. Let's build a model!

Procedure

- Using the marker, number the cups 1, 2, and 3.

- Following the directions on the package, mix ½ cup of plaster of Paris with the specified amount of water. Stir it well until you have a smooth, creamy mix.

- Arrange layers of gravel, sand, clay, and plaster in each cup according to the following table. The material at the bottom of the cup should match the material at the bottom of the table. The plaster layers should be about 1–2 cm thick. The other layers should be 2–4 cm thick. Be sure that no layer leaves any openings at the edges of the cup.

Cup 1	Cup 2	Cup 3
gravel	plaster	plaster
sand	clay	sand
plaster	sand	clay
clay	gravel	gravel

- Allow the cups to stand until the plaster hardens.

When rainwater hits the ground, it passes through the soil to the groundwater system below. This process of seeping downward is called *percolation*. If the water encounters a material that is solid (no holes), it won't pass any farther into the ground. Materials that stop water are described as *impermeable*.

If the material has holes (pores), the water *might* pass through it. These kinds of materials are called *porous*. However, if the pores are not connected to each other or are too small, the material will be impermeable even though it's not solid.

Goals

After completing this lab, you will be able to
- ✓ define porosity and permeability.
- ✓ explain how some porous materials store water.
- ✓ explain how impermeable materials trap water.
- ✓ model the groundwater system.

Equipment

clear plastic cups (3)
marker
pea-sized gravel
sand
clay
plaster of Paris
disposable mixing container and spoon
flat-bladed screwdriver

Plaster Safety

Plaster of Paris is a useful and fun material for science as well as art. But you need to handle it carefully. As plaster hardens, it gives off heat. Chemists call this kind of chemical reaction *exothermic*. Never coat any part of your body with plaster. And never try to make molds of your hands by plunging them into a container of hardening plaster. Students have gotten severe burns and even lost fingers by doing this!

Never dump liquid plaster down the sink. Plaster hardens in pipes, producing very hard-to-clear blockages. Allow unused plaster to harden. Then throw it in the trash.

Figure 1 Pumice is porous but impermeable.

If the material is porous and the holes are connected together, water can pass through the material. This kind of material is *permeable*. Permeable materials allow water to pass through them. They can also store water in their pores, just as a sponge does.

- Let's make a few predictions before we test our model. Look at each row in the table below. Mark an *X* in each column that you think applies to a layer of the material.

Material	Porous	Non-porous	Permeable	Impermeable
gravel				
plaster				
sand				
clay				

- It's time to percolate! Fill the cups with water to within 1 cm of the top.

- Watch the water as it percolates down through the layers. In the Trial 1 column of the table below, record the layers that the water reaches in each cup. If a layer stops the water flow, include it in the list.

- Using the screwdriver, carefully crack the plaster layer in cups 2 and 3. In the Trial 2 column, record the layers that the water reaches *after* you crack the plaster.

Cup	Trial 1	Trial 2
1		
2		
3		

1. How accurate were your predictions for each layer's behavior in both trials?

_____

2. Which materials can store water? trap water?

_____

3. What kind of water table does cup 3 model *after* you crack the plaster? Explain why. (*Hint*: Review Subsection 17.4 in your textbook.)

_____

_____

4. What kind of rock does plaster model? Explain why. Be sure to discuss the cracks that you made in the plaster.

_____

_____

17B Taking the Waters

Water picks up minerals as it moves through the ground. The presence of these minerals in water can be either desirable or undesirable. Since we need minerals for our bodies to function properly, drinking mineral water can benefit our health.

Europeans have been "taking the waters" at spas for centuries. Today, we can purchase mineral water bottled at its source. Although potentially healthful, waters with a high mineral content may taste terrible, smell unpleasant, or cause soap to form a sticky scum rather than lather. For reasons such as these, water companies may adjust mineral content during the water purification process.

Water that contains high concentrations of dissolved minerals is called *hard water*, while water that contains low concentrations is called *soft water*. Minerals that commonly cause hard water are calcium or magnesium compounds. These compounds may be further classified as carbonates, sulfates, or chlorides. As your textbook explains, there are a number of methods for reducing (softening) the mineral content of water. Let's explore hard and soft water to see what it's like and how it behaves.

Procedure

- Pour a sample of the mineral water into a clean disposable cup. Pour a sample of distilled water into another cup. Smell and then taste each sample. Record your impressions in the table below.

Sample	Odor	Taste
Mineral water		
Distilled water		

- Fill the four test tubes about half full with the following types of water: distilled, tap, mineral, and distilled. Add a small pinch of Epsom salts to the distilled water in the last tube. **Don't taste the water after you put it in the test tubes!**

- Add *one* drop of liquid soap to the first tube.

- Stopper the tube or hold your thumb over the end. Shake the tube vigorously for 10 seconds. Place the tube in the test tube rack.

- Wait one minute. Measure the height between the water level and the top of the suds to the nearest 0.1 cm. Record the height in the table on the next page.

- Repeat the previous three steps for each of the remaining tubes.

name_____

section_____ date_____

Goals

After completing this lab, you will be able to
- ✓ define hard and soft water.
- ✓ measure water hardness.
- ✓ list uses of hard and soft water.
- ✓ describe the effects dissolved minerals have on water's hardness and flavor.

Equipment

disposable cups (2)
large test tubes (4)
test tube stoppers (4)
test tube rack
centimeter ruler
distilled water
mineral water
liquid soap
Epsom salts (magnesium sulfate heptahydrate)

Figure 1 The mineral waters at Bath, England, are famous. However, many people think they taste terrible!

Figure 2 Checking water hardness

Water Type	Suds Height (cm)
Distilled	
Tap	
Mineral	
Distilled + Epsom salts	

1. Which water sample produced the tallest layer of suds?

_____

2. Is the distilled water hard or soft? Explain why.

_____

_____

3. Was the tap water hard or soft?

_____

4. Is the distilled water/Epsom salts mixture hard or soft? Explain why.

_____

_____

5. Does distilled water taste pleasant? Explain why or why not.

_____

_____

6. Aside from the possible health benefits, why is mineral water usually better to drink than distilled water? What causes this advantage?

_____

_____

7. When would mineral water be unpleasant to drink? Give an example.

_____

_____

8. Why is soap useful as an indicator of water hardness?

_____

_____

9. Where in your home would it be especially beneficial to use soft water?

_____

_____

18 EARTH'S ATMOSPHERE

18A Weighty Matters

name_____

section_____ date_____

Have you ever heard the expression "light as air"? This phrase reflects a view that many people hold even today in the twenty-first century. In fact, through most of history, philosophers and scientists thought that air didn't weigh anything at all. Besides that, until the 1600s, many believed that a vacuum couldn't exist!

As you've learned in your textbook, the earth's atmosphere is made up of a mixture of gases, mostly nitrogen and oxygen. And as you should remember from Chapter 2, all matter has mass. So logically, the atmosphere can't be weightless. In fact, air can be pretty heavy.

During the mid-1600s, scientists began to try to find out if air had weight and if a vacuum could be produced. As they performed their experiments, they created an instrument for measuring the weight of the earth's atmosphere. Today, we call that instrument a *barometer*.

As you'll learn in the next chapter, the weight of the earth's atmosphere changes with the weather. Barometers measure these changes. It wasn't until the 1800s, however, that scientists began to use barometers to help predict the weather. In this lab, you're going to build a simple barometer and use it to monitor the weather.

Procedure

- Fill the thermos with warm tap water.
- Carefully insert the glass tube through the stopper, leaving about 1 cm protruding from the small end. You should lubricate the end of the tube with glycerin first and wear protective gloves when inserting the tube.
- Fill the beaker with 40 mL of room-temperature water. Add a drop of food coloring and stir.
- Empty the warm water from the thermos and quickly insert the stopper.
- Invert the thermos and place the end of the tube in the beaker of water.
- Secure the upside-down thermos with the ring stand and clamp while keeping the end of the tube in the beaker of water.

As the air inside the thermos cools, it contracts, creating a partial vacuum. The atmosphere's weight will push some of the water in the beaker up the tube. When the atmosphere's pressure matches the pressure in the thermos, the water will stop rising.

Goals

After completing this lab, you will be able to
✓ explain how a barometer works.
✓ build and calibrate a simple barometer.
✓ relate barometric pressure to weather.

Equipment

small, narrow-mouth thermos
1-hole rubber stopper to fit thermos
glass tube to fit stopper, 40 cm
ring stand with large clamp
beaker, 50 mL
food coloring
paper ruler template (available on the Teacher's Toolkit CD and on the EARTH SCIENCE 4th Edition Resources webpage)
glycerin
protective gloves
colored pens or pencils
graph paper (provided)

Figure 1 Although Evangelista Torricelli (1608–47) is credited with inventing the barometer in 1643, several scientists contributed to its development.

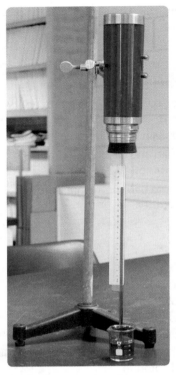

Figure 2 The completed barometer

Unit Confusion

Barometric pressure units can be confusing! Depending on where you live, weather services will use one of several different units. Commercially made barometers may also report pressure in one of several different units. Examples include inches of mercury (inHg), millibars (mb), hectopascals (hPa), or centimeters of mercury (cmHg).

- If the water rises all the way to the top of the tube, the vacuum in the thermos is too great. Repeat the procedure using water that is cooler. This will reduce the vacuum produced when the thermos cools.
- Place the barometer in a location with a fairly constant temperature. Be sure it's not near a window or an air conditioner/heat duct. Let it sit overnight so that it adjusts to the room's conditions.
- The next day, tape the paper ruler to the glass tube so the middle of the ruler is aligned with the water level in the tube.
- In the table below, record to the nearest 1 mm the position of the water level on the ruler.
- Using a commercial barometer or an online weather service, obtain the "official" barometric pressure. Record this value in the table. Include the pressure unit that the barometer or service uses.
- Record the date and a brief description of the current weather conditions.
- Repeat the previous three steps every day for a total of five days.
- Every day, check the water level in the beaker. If it drops due to evaporation, add water to the beaker to maintain a constant quantity.

Date	Your Barometer (mm)	Official Pressure	Weather

- Using the graphing area on page 166, plot the two sets of data (your barometer and the official pressure). The *x*-axis represents the day number. Create a suitable scale for the official pressure on the left *y*-axis. Create a suitable scale for your barometer on the right *y*-axis. Plot the two sets of data and draw straight lines between the points of each set. Use different colors for each plot and draw a short color line in the legend box to identify each plot.

1. Did your barometer show the same *trend* as the official one?

2. Will an increase in atmospheric pressure make the water level in the tube rise or fall? Explain why.

name _____

_____

_____

3. How did your pressure readings compare to those from the "official" source?

_____

4. Was there any relationship between the day's weather and the barometric pressure? Explain.

_____

_____

_____

5. What effect would a change in room temperature, *without* a change in the atmosphere's pressure, have on the water level in the tube? Explain.

_____

_____

_____

6. What would happen if the thermos lost its partial vacuum? Explain.

_____

_____

_____

7. For many years, mercury was the liquid of choice for barometers. Mercury is almost 14 times denser than water. If you replaced the water in your barometer with mercury, what would change?

_____

_____

_____

Dangerous but Useful

The chemical element mercury (Hg) is one of the few metals that can be liquid at or near room temperature. Its high density makes it useful in a variety of scientific instruments and applications. But mercury can be highly toxic under certain conditions. For this reason, relatively few scientific instruments use mercury nowadays.

Barometric Pressure Comparison

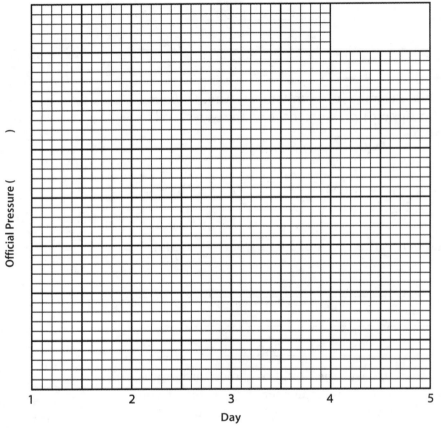

Official Pressure (   )

My Barometer (mm)

Day

18B Warming Up

name_____

section_____ date_____

We all know that standing in the sun on a cold day makes you feel warmer. Solar energy makes some things heat up. But we also know that some materials reflect solar energy away, keeping them cool. Think of the shiny sunshades that you put under the windshield of your car on a hot day.

As you learned in Subsection 18.10 of your textbook, 1367 W of energy falls on each square meter of the earth's outer atmosphere. About 60–75% of this energy actually gets to the ground. The energy warms the earth and, more importantly, energizes the atmosphere. And, as you will learn in the next chapter, this makes weather happen.

In this lab, you're going to explore how solar energy behaves when it encounters different materials. You'll also measure the solar constant at your location. Let's get warmed up!

Procedure

- Fill one of the paper cups with water to within 1 cm of the rim. Pour the water into the graduated cylinder. Record the volume of water in the graduated cylinder rounded to the nearest division on the cylinder. Discard the water.

_____

- Measure the diameter of the top of the paper cup to the nearest 0.1 cm. Then convert the number to *meters* and record it.

_____

- Number the *foam* cups 1, 2, 3, and 4. Spray the inside of each *paper* cup with the black paint. Let them dry overnight. Then insert them into the foam cups.

- Fill the cardboard box with the insulating material.

- Nestle the four cups into the insulation so they are well protected.

- Find a sunny spot outside. Measure the air temperature with a thermometer. Keep the thermometer shaded by your body so it's not in direct sunlight. Record the temperature to the nearest 1 °C.

_____

- At a water faucet, adjust the hot and cold water mixture until the temperature is the same as the air temperature that you just measured. Once you get the temperature correct, fill the 1 L beaker with water.

Goals

After completing this lab, you will be able to

✓ compare the effects of different materials on solar energy collection.

✓ explain the greenhouse effect.

✓ measure the local solar constant.

Equipment

shallow cardboard box
paper coffee cups (4)
foam coffee cups (4)
flat black spray paint
lab thermometers (4)
clear plastic wrap
aluminum foil
small glass plate
centimeter ruler
red, green, and blue food coloring
large graduated cylinder or measuring cup
beaker, 1 L
loose insulating material

Figure 1 Solar panels convert some of the solar energy that reaches the earth's surface into electricity.

© 2012 BJU Press. Reproduction prohibited.

Basic Black

You may be wondering why we've painted the cups black and dyed the water. As you probably know from experience, dark colors tend to absorb more energy from sunlight than light colors do. Think about how hot an asphalt pavement gets on a sunny day. The reason is simple: dark colors absorb most of the energy and reflect back only a small amount. Light colors do the opposite.

Figure 2 Solar experiment setup

- Add several drops of each color of food coloring to the water. You want the water to be as dark as possible.
- Fill each cup with the dark water to within 1 cm of the rim.
- Cover the top of cup 1 with plastic wrap. Cover the top of cup 2 with aluminum foil. Cover the top of cup 3 with the glass plate. Cup 4 will be open to the air.
- Carefully carry the box to the sunny spot you picked earlier. Have several people stand so that they shade the box from the sunlight. If you can't cast a shadow on the box, have two people hold a sheet of newspaper over the box so that it's shaded.
- Poke a hole in the plastic wrap and foil on cups 1 and 2. Slide the glass plate covering cup 3 slightly to one side so that there's a small gap.
- Insert a thermometer all the way into each cup. Wait one minute for them to adjust, and read the temperature in each cup. These will be the experiment's start temperatures. Record the temperatures to the nearest 1 °C in the table below. Leave the thermometers in place.
- Move away from the box so that it's now in full sunlight. Make a note of the time.
- After five minutes, gently stir the water in each cup by jiggling the thermometers.
- Every five minutes, stir the water again. When a total of 30 minutes has passed, record the temperatures to the nearest 1 °C in the table.
- Go back inside and calculate the temperature change in each cup by subtracting the start temperature from the end temperature ($t_{end} - t_{start}$). Record the temperature changes in the table.

Cup	Start Temperature (°C)	End Temperature (°C)	Temperature Change (°C)
1 (plastic)			
2 (foil)			
3 (glass)			
4 (open)			

1. How do the temperature changes in the four cups compare?

_____

_____

_____

2. The plastic wrap and the glass plate allow visible and some ultraviolet light through, but they tend to block infrared light. Explain what caused the temperature difference between the four cups.

name _____

_____

_____

_____

3. What real-world effect do the plastic wrap and the glass plate model? (*Hint*: Review Subsection 18.12 in your textbook.)

_____

The *solar constant* is a measure of the energy hitting a given area of the earth's surface. Let's see what the solar constant is at the location where you performed your tests. We'll use cup 4's temperature change to calculate it.

- Calculate the area of the cup's opening using the following formula, round it to three decimal places, and record it.

$$A = \pi \times \frac{d^2}{4}.$$

> **Pi Anyone?**
>
> If your calculator doesn't have a π key, substitute the number 3.14.

_____

- Calculate and record the mass of the water based on the volume you measured earlier. Remember, 1 mL of water has a mass of 1 g.

_____

If you completed Lab 4A, you remember that energy is measured in joules (J). It takes 4.18 J of energy to raise the temperature of 1 g of water by 1 °C. We already know the mass of the water and the temperature change, so we can calculate the energy absorbed by the water.

- Calculate the energy (*E*) absorbed by the water with the following formula, round it to the nearest 1 J, and record it.

$E = 4.18 \text{ J/g} \cdot {}^\circ\text{C} \times \text{water mass (g)} \times \text{temperature change (°C)}.$

_____

- We're now ready to calculate the local solar constant. To do this, we must know the energy absorbed, the area of the surface, and the time. We've calculated the first two values, and we know the third (30 min = 1800 s). The unit for the solar constant is watts per square meter (W/m²). Calculate the solar constant with the following equation, round it to the nearest 1 W/m², and record it.

$$\text{solar constant} = \frac{E\ (\text{J})}{A\ (\text{m}^2) \times 1800\ \text{s}}.$$

_____

- Let's see how much energy actually reached you from space. We know that 1367 W/m² is striking the upper atmosphere. Calculate the percent that reached the ground with the following formula, round it to the nearest 1%, and record it.

$$\% \text{ energy} = \frac{\text{local solar constant (W/m}^2)}{1367\ \text{W/m}^2} \times 100\%.$$

_____

4. If you were planning to install solar collectors on your house, why would it be a good idea to determine the local solar constant first?

_____

_____

_____

5. Why was it necessary to insulate the cups for this experiment?

_____

_____

6. Why was it necessary to adjust the initial water temperature to that of the air?

_____

_____

_____

19 WEATHER

19A On the Wings of the Wind

name_____

section_____   date_____

"How fast is the wind blowing?" If someone asked you that question, you probably couldn't answer exactly. You might say something like, "It's really windy today," but that's the best you could do. Our general impressions of natural events are interesting, but they're not very useful if we're doing science. Science works with data, and the most useful kind of data is *measured data*. Most measured data comes from instruments and takes the form of numbers.

Scientists prefer measured data for another reason. In theory, every scientist should get the same result if he measures the same thing with the same instrument. This principle is called *repeatability*. Of course, it's not possible to share one instrument among many scientists, but if each scientist uses an "identical" instrument, he should get the same results.

Scientists who study the atmosphere need to know how fast the wind is blowing. But how do we turn the motion of the air into a number? We use an instrument that converts one quantity (the rate of air movement) into another that we can measure. You're going to build an instrument called a *tilting plate anemometer* (Gk. *anemos*—wind + Gk. *metron*—measure) that will turn the air movement into a number that represents the *wind speed*.

Procedure

- Using the scissors, cut out the two patterns from the anemometer template.

- Glue each pattern to the sheet of foamcore. Let the glue dry.

- Carefully cut out the two pieces using the utility knife and the metal ruler. *Be careful not to cut yourself or the table.* The curved section is called the *body*, while the T-shaped section is called the *tilting plate*.

- Straighten out the paper clip so you have a piece of stiff wire. Use the wire to punch through the dot marked on the body section of the anemometer. Remove the wire.

- Carefully push the wire through the foam between the paper layers on one side of the tilting plate section at the location marked on the pattern. Insert the body section in the slot and pass the wire through the punched hole. Push the wire through the foam on the other side of the tilting plate section. The tilting plate should swing freely on the wire.

- Tape the dowel rod or pencil along the foam edge of the body section labeled **Support**. You will use the rod as a handle to hold the instrument.

Goals

After completing this lab, you will be able to

✓ describe how a tilting plate anemometer measures wind speed.

✓ build and calibrate an anemometer.

✓ explain how calibrated instruments provide repeatability in scientific measurements.

Equipment

anemometer template (available on the Teacher's Toolkit CD and on the *EARTH SCIENCE* 4th Edition Resources webpage)

foamcore sheet (¼ in.), 6 × 8 in. or larger

metal ruler

scissors

utility knife

paper clip

glue stick

masking tape

modeling clay

new pencil or ¼ in. dowel rod, 8 in. long

graph paper (provided)

Figure 1 The completed anemometer

Your anemometer will measure the wind speed when you hold it with the tilting plate facing straight into the wind. The amount that the plate tilts corresponds to the wind speed.

1. Explain how the anemometer works.

_____

_____

_____

The anemometer has a scale printed on the curved section (0–16), but the scale doesn't actually mean anything. The numbers just tell you how much the plate tilts. They don't tell you how fast the wind is blowing in useful units like kilometers per hour (km/h). To turn the scale into real units, we have to figure out how many km/h each number on the scale represents. We call this process *calibration*.

To calibrate an instrument, you compare it to another instrument that reports the units you need. If you completed Lab 18A, you did something similar when you calibrated your barometer. In this case, you will use a car speedometer as the calibration instrument. Calibrate the anemometer as follows.

- Sit in the front passenger seat and hold the anemometer out the window. To protect your hand from injury, don't stick it out farther than the width of the side view mirror. Be sure the mirror does not block the wind from the anemometer. Avoid calibrating the anemometer on a windy day!

- Have the driver slowly speed up to 40 km/h (25 mi/h). Note how much the plate tilts. It should tilt no higher than the top number on the scale (16). If it tilts too far, add a glob of modeling clay to the front of the plate at the location labeled **Weight** so it requires more force to tilt the plate.

- Have the driver carefully adjust the car's speed to each value shown in the table below. Write down the scale value that the plate tilts to at each of these speeds.

Speed (mi/h)	Speed (km/h)	Scale Value
0	0	0
4	5	
7	10	
10	15	
13	20	
16	25	
19	30	
22	35	
25	40	

This table is a good start, but you need to do one more thing before your anemometer is fully calibrated. You need to draw a graph called a *calibration curve*. If you completed Lab 11A, you should remember calibration curves.

name_____

- Using the graphing area on the next page, plot the calibration data. The *x*-axis represents the scale values and the *y*-axis represents the actual speeds (in km/h).

- Draw a smooth curve between the points.

The calibration curve allows you to translate any scale value into a real speed. For example, let's say that you take your anemometer outside on a windy day. The plate tilts to 12 on the scale. To convert this value into km/h, just find 12 on the *x*-axis and move straight up until you reach the calibration curve. Move left until you come to the *y*-axis. The value at this location is your actual wind speed in km/h.

2. Take a look at your calibration curve. Is it a straight line?

_____

3. Does the calibration curve have to be a straight line to be useful? Explain.

_____

_____

_____

4. Two people build identical anemometers and calibrate them using the same car speedometer. If they measure the same wind, should they get the same results? Explain why or why not.

_____

_____

_____

5. Two people build different kinds of anemometers but they calibrate them with the same standard instrument (the same speedometer). If they measure the same wind, should they get the same results? Explain why or why not.

_____

_____

_____

6. What is the key to repeatability in scientific instruments?

_____

_____

_____

Anemometer Calibration

19B Psyched Out

name _____

section _____ date _____

"It's not the heat; it's the humidity!" Have you ever heard someone make that complaint? If so, you've come in contact with a key weather principle. Humidity plays a major role in comfort. People can tolerate hot days better if the air is dry. But a hot, humid day makes us just plain miserable.

As your textbook explains, relative humidity (RH) is the amount of water in the air relative to the amount that the air can hold at a given temperature. Warm air can hold more moisture than cool air can. So 75% RH on a hot day means a much higher *absolute humidity* than 75% RH on a cold day. Our bodies cool themselves by evaporating perspiration. So when it's very humid, we can't evaporate enough perspiration to stay comfortable.

Measuring humidity is not easy! We use *hygrometers* to measure it, and there are many different types. In this lab, you're going to build a type of hygrometer called a *sling psychrometer* (Gk. *psukhro*—cold + Gk. *metron*—measure). As its name implies, it measures cooling to help determine relative humidity.

Procedure

- Using the foam tape, secure the two thermometers together back-to-back. Be sure the holes at the top line up. Do not press the thermometers together too hard, or you'll crack the glass tubes!

- Insert the screw through the holes and screw it into the end of the dowel rod. Do not tighten it all the way. You should be able to spin the thermometers by holding the dowel rod like a handle.

- Cut and fold the gauze into a square double layer large enough to cover one thermometer bulb. Place the gauze pad on top of the outside thermometer bulb (the one opposite the handle). Wrap two rubber bands around both thermometers to help hold the gauze in place. The thermometer wrapped in gauze is called the *wet-bulb thermometer*. The other thermometer is called the *dry-bulb thermometer*.

- Wet the gauze with room-temperature water. Spin the psychrometer by the handle for one minute. Be careful not to hit anyone!

- Read both thermometers immediately after you've finished spinning them. Record the temperatures to the nearest 1 °C in the table on the next page.

- Subtract the wet-bulb temperature from the dry ($t_D - t_W$) and record the difference in the table.

- Go to Appendix L in the back of your textbook. The chart helps you convert temperatures to relative humidity.

Goals

After completing this lab, you will be able to
✓ build a sling psychrometer.
✓ use a psychrometer to measure relative humidity.
✓ explain how a psychrometer works.
✓ relate relative humidity to cooling and comfort.

Equipment

mounted outdoor thermometers (2)
dowel rod ¾ in. diameter, 2 in. long
¾ in. #8 pan-head screw
screwdriver
scissors
double-sided foam tape
gauze square
rubber bands (2)

Figure 1 The finished psychrometer

Scientific Symbols

Scientists frequently use symbols to represent quantities.
t_D = dry-bulb temperature
t_W = wet-bulb temperature

- Find the dry-bulb temperature in the column along the left side of the table.
- Find the temperature difference between the two thermometers in the row along the top of the table.
- Locate the number at the intersection of the row and column temperatures. This number is the relative humidity in percent. Record it in the table. For example, if the dry bulb reads 27 °C and the temperature difference is 14 °C, the relative humidity is 16%.
- Measure the relative humidity for five days and record it in the table.

Day	Dry Bulb (°C)	Wet Bulb (°C)	Difference (°C)	RH (%)
1				
2				
3				
4				
5				

1. In most cases, the wet-bulb temperature will be lower than the dry. Explain why. (*Hint*: Think of how your body cools itself.)

   _____

   _____

   _____

2. What would make the wet-bulb temperature significantly colder than the dry?

   _____

   _____

   _____

3. You spin the psychrometer for one minute and find that both thermometers read the same. What is the relative humidity? How do you know?

   _____

   _____

   _____

4. In a few sentences, explain how a psychrometer measures relative humidity. Be sure to include the reason for spinning it for one minute.

name_____

_____

_____

_____

5. Why does a fan make you cooler on a hot day? Does it actually change the temperature of the air around you?

_____

_____

_____

6. Under what conditions will a fan *not* make you any cooler? Explain why.

_____

_____

_____

7. People who live in dry climates like that of Arizona can live comfortably at fairly high temperatures. Explain the reason.

_____

_____

_____

8. Can you think of a danger to people who live in hot, dry climates? Explain the cause of the danger.

_____

_____

_____

20 STORMS AND WEATHER PREDICTION

20A Tornado Chasing

name_____

section_____   date_____

Would you like to chase a tornado? Weather scientists monitor tornadoes from special armored vehicles. Some people chase storms recreationally, hoping to see a tornado. This activity is pretty dangerous, and there's no guarantee of seeing a tornado. In this lab, you're going to chase about 100 tornadoes and never leave your computer to do it!

Knowing what to do when a tornado strikes can save your life. However, a lot of tornado safety advice is just folklore. Indeed, some "safety" tips can *increase* your chance of injury during a tornado. One popular piece of advice suggests going to a basement (a good idea!) and crouching in the *southwest* corner. Why the southwest corner? Many people believe that tornadoes always move from southwest to northeast. They assume that if the building is hit, the debris will be blown away from them.

Detailed studies in the 1960s and 1970s revealed that the southwest corner is actually the *most* likely part of a house to be destroyed if a tornado is moving from southwest to northeast. But do tornadoes always move in this way? And if so, is there an "ideal" safe location inside a building?

Online GIS resources allow us to study historical tornadoes and analyze their behavior. Using these tools, we can model tornado paths and discover whether tornadoes move predictably or not. Let's chase some tornadoes!

Goals

After completing this lab, you will be able to
- ✓ model tornado behavior using GIS resources.
- ✓ evaluate a common tornado safety tip.

Equipment

computer with Internet access
graph paper (provided)

Figure 1 Scientists use special vehicles to "chase" tornadoes.

Procedure

- Your teacher will direct you to an online tornado history database. We want to collect path data for about 100 tornadoes.

1. Why is it important to collect data from so many tornadoes?

_____

_____

- Tornadoes occur most frequently in the middle section of the United States. Indeed, many people call this part of the country "Tornado Alley." Illinois is a good choice for this lab because it's near Tornado Alley and experiences a lot of tornadoes. But it doesn't have so many that they're hard to tell apart. On the Tornado History Project webpage, select "Illinois" as the **State**.

- Select a **Fujita** number of 2. Leave all other boxes set to **Any**. Click the **Submit** button.

New and Improved?

Until 2007, weather scientists rated tornado strength using the Fujita-Pearson (F) scale. Starting in 2007, this scale was replaced by the *Enhanced Fujita* (EF) scale. Both scales rate tornadoes from 0 to 5, with 5 being the most powerful. The EF scale uses different ways for calculating tornado strength. Its estimated wind speeds are also slightly different. But the scales are similar enough that they mean almost the same thing. Tornadoes cataloged before 2007 are still rated using the original F scale, which is the reason tornado databases often use this scale instead of the newer EF scale.

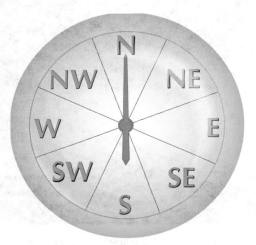

Figure 2 Path direction guide

2. Why did we pick F2 for our tornado type? (*Hint*: See Appendix M in the textbook.)

_____

_____

- Using the map's zoom and position controls, zoom in close enough to see the individual tornadoes at the top of the state. A cone-shaped tornado icon identifies the tornado's touchdown point, and the colored line indicates its path.

- Starting at the top of the state and working downward, look at each tornado and determine the compass direction of its path. Use the direction guide provided in the margin to help you choose the correct compass direction. If a tornado doesn't follow a straight line, use the longest part of its path to determine the direction.

- Once you determine the tornado's direction, draw a tally mark in the correct row of the table below. Collect data from about 50 tornadoes.

- Do another search in Illinois with the **Fujita** number set to 3. Collect path data from another 50 tornadoes. Add it to the data already in the table.

3. Why did we add F3 data to our F2 data?

_____

_____

Direction	Number of Tornadoes
N	
NE	
E	
SE	
S	
SW	
W	
NW	

- Using the graphing area on page 182, create a histogram to model tornado direction. You may wish to review histograms from Lab 1B. The bar height for each path direction should equal the tally number from the matching row in the table.

- Look at your model and try to determine the overall trend of tornado behavior.

4. Do all tornadoes travel from southwest to northeast?

_____

_____

5. Is there any truth to the belief that tornadoes travel from southwest to northeast? Explain.

_____

_____

6. Are there directions that tornadoes rarely, if ever, travel? Explain.

_____

_____

After the studies of the 1960s and 1970s, scientists changed their safety recommendations. Instead of telling people to go to the southwest corner of their basements, they advised them to go to the corner *opposite* to the tornado's approach direction.

7. Based on your model, do you think people should always go to the *northeast* corner of a basement? Explain.

_____

_____

8. Would it be a good idea to go outside, observe an oncoming tornado, determine its path, and then choose the best corner of a basement? Explain.

_____

_____

Today, most experts agree that it's crucial to shelter in the strongest part of a building, usually a basement or inner room without windows. Getting under something sturdy like a work-bench or stairway can enhance your safety.

9. Why should we study tornadoes and try to develop safety strategies that improve people's survival?

_____

_____

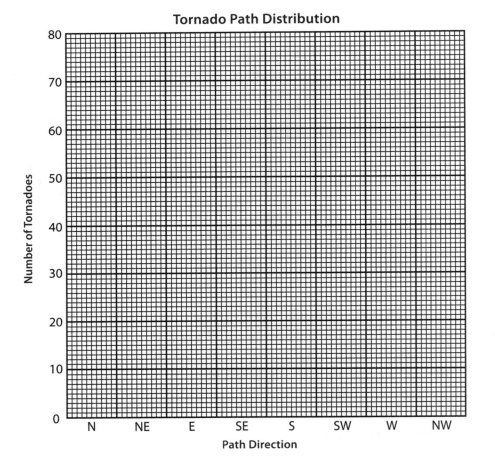

Tornado Path Distribution

20B Hurricane Hunting

Flying in a Hurricane Hunter plane is probably one of the most exciting scientific adventures. And it's incredibly useful too. Thanks to the wealth of data these planes gather, scientists are beginning to understand the forces that shape, control, and dissipate these ferocious tropical cyclones.

The National Hurricane Center, part of the National Weather Service, maintains a huge database of historical hurricane information. From it, scientists have constructed computer models that help predict the behavior of future tropical cyclones. These models have gotten good enough that people in endangered areas can be warned to evacuate in plenty of time. Thanks to them, many lives have been saved.

In this lab, you're going to do some slightly less dramatic hurricane hunting. You're going to examine the behavior of two storms. The first one, Katrina (2005), was the costliest hurricane in US history to date with damages reaching $91.5 billion. Katrina also claimed 1836 lives. The second storm, Matthew (2004), never developed into a full hurricane. Its damages came to about $361,000, and no lives were lost.

These storms occurred just one year apart and in the same part of the world. Yet their effects were totally different. What made the difference? Let's get tracking and find out!

Procedure

- Hurricane scientists track a tropical cyclone by plotting its position on a map hour by hour. They also classify its current stage of development. A hurricane's stage depends on its maximum rotational wind speed. The following table shows the classification system.

Stage	Wind Speed (km/h)	Color Code
Tropical Depression (TD)	≤ 62	(cyan)
Tropical Storm (TS)	63–118	(green)
Category 1 (H1)	119–153	(yellow)
Category 2 (H2)	154–177	(orange)
Category 3 (H3)	178–209	(red)
Category 4 (H4)	210–249	(magenta)
Category 5 (H5)	≥ 250	(purple)

name _____

section _____   date _____

Goals

After completing this lab, you will be able to

✓ plot the path of a hurricane.

✓ explain the causes for change in a hurricane's strength.

Equipment

colored pen or pencil set
ruler

Figure 1 A NOAA Hurricane Hunter plane flies into the eye of Hurricane Katrina.

Extras

Hurricane data tables often include an additional category called *Extratropical* (ET). This category is *not* based on a cyclone's wind speed. Instead, a cyclone is classified as extratropical when it's outside the tropics and gets its energy from different sources than tropical cyclones do. Many hurricanes and tropical storms become extratropical at the end of their existence as they move northward out of the tropics. Extratropical cyclones can have any wind speed. Generally, when a storm moves above lat. 30°N, it becomes extratropical.

- Examine the two tables that follow on the next page. Each row represents the storm's position, wind speed, and development stage at a given time. Notice that the observation times are recorded in 24-hour format.

- Using the map on page 186, plot each storm's track by placing a colored dot at the proper latitude/longitude coordinates. Plot each position to the nearest 1°. The dot's color should indicate the storm's development stage. Use the colors from the table on the previous page.

- Draw a smooth line between the points to show the storm's track from its beginning to the point where it dissipates. Label each track with the storm's name.

1. In which body of water did Hurricane Katrina obtain most of its energy? How do you know?

   _____

   _____

   _____

2. What is one possible reason that Katrina remained fairly weak until after August 25?

   _____

   _____

3. Hurricane Katrina did an immense amount of damage to the city of New Orleans in Louisiana. Can you explain why?

   _____

   _____

   _____

4. In which part of the country did Hurricane Katrina lose its identity and become an ordinary storm?

   _____

   _____

5. Tropical Storm Matthew never actually became a hurricane. Suggest some reasons why not.

   _____

   _____

   _____

6. Tropical Storm Matthew came ashore close to the same place as Hurricane Katrina, yet it caused minimal damage. Explain why.

_____

_____

_____

7. After which date do you think Hurricane Katrina could have been reclassified as extratropical (ET)? Explain why.

_____

_____

_____

8. The thick red line in the Gulf of Mexico on the map marks the location of a warm ocean current known as the *Loop Current*. Explain its possible role in Hurricane Katrina's development.

_____

_____

_____

9. Why are hurricane tracking, data collection, and computer modeling so important to exercising wise dominion?

_____

_____

_____

name_____

Hurricane Katrina (2005)

Date	Time	Latitude	Longitude	Speed (km/h)	Stage
Aug 23	1800	23.1 N	75.1 W	56	TD
Aug 24	0600	23.8 N	76.2 W	56	TD
Aug 24	1800	25.4 N	76.9 W	74	TS
Aug 25	0600	26.1 N	78.4 W	93	TS
Aug 25	1800	26.2 N	79.6 W	111	TS
Aug 26	0600	25.4 N	81.3 W	120	H1
Aug 26	1800	24.9 N	82.6 W	157	H2
Aug 27	0600	24.4 N	84.0 W	176	H2
Aug 27	1800	24.5 N	85.3 W	185	H3
Aug 28	0600	25.2 N	86.7 W	232	H4
Aug 28	1800	26.3 N	88.6 W	278	H5
Aug 29	0600	28.2 N	89.6 W	232	H4
Aug 29	1800	31.1 N	89.6 W	148	H1
Aug 30	0600	34.1 N	88.6 W	74	TS
Aug 30	1800	37.0 N	87.0 W	56	TD
Aug 31	0600	40.1 N	82.9 W	46	TD

http://www.csc.noaa.gov/hurricanes

Tropical Storm Matthew (2004)

Date	Time	Latitude	Longitude	Speed (km/h)	Stage
Oct 8	1200	24.0 N	95.4 W	56	TD
Oct 8	1800	24.1 N	94.2 W	65	TS
Oct 9	0000	24.6 N	93.7 W	74	TS
Oct 9	0600	25.3 N	93.2 W	65	TS
Oct 9	1200	26.3 N	92.8 W	65	TS
Oct 9	1800	26.8 N	92.0 W	74	TS
Oct 10	0000	27.3 N	91.4 W	74	TS
Oct 10	0600	28.1 N	91.2 W	74	TS
Oct 10	1200	29.4 N	90.9 W	56	TD
Oct 10	1800	30.4 N	90.9 W	46	TD
Oct 11	0000	32.0 N	91.0 W	46	TD
Oct 11	0600	33.6 N	91.9 W	37	TD

http://www.csc.noaa.gov/hurricanes

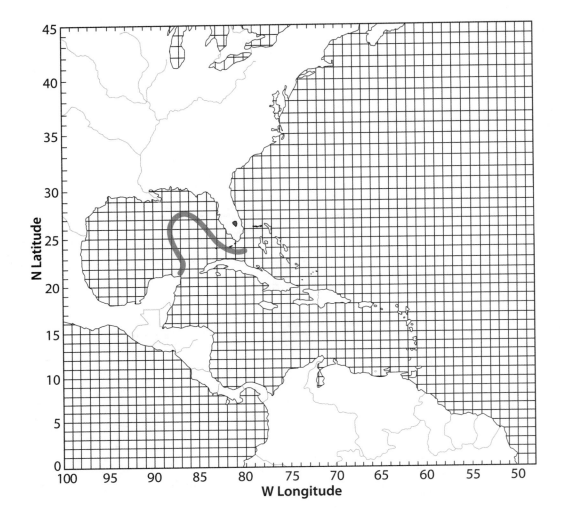

21 CLIMATE AND CLIMATE CHANGE

21A Too Complex

name _____

section _____ date _____

How hard is it to predict your next report card grade in this class? Hopefully, not too difficult! By now you probably realize that your final grade is made up of a few dozen grades from home-work assignments, quizzes, tests, and projects. If you know how well you've been doing, you can predict your future grade with reasonable accuracy.

But what if someone asks you to predict whether it will be sunny or rainy five years from now? You would quite correctly say that predicting the weather that far in the future is very difficult. But what makes it difficult? The answer is *complexity*.

Many different factors combine to shape the weather. The sun powers the weather, but the sun changes from day to day. Sometimes the sun has storms on its surface, and sometimes it's quiet. The oceans store and release heat, but they move all the time. The atmosphere also moves constantly and contains dif-ferent amounts of moisture every hour. Human-built structures alter the flow of air over the surface of the land. These, and many other factors, determine whether the day will be rainy, stormy, sunny, or cloudy.

If just a few factors controlled the weather, making a long-range prediction wouldn't be too hard. But more than just a few factors influence the weather. How many factors must you have before things get too complex? Let's find out by creating a tasty model.

Goals

After completing this lab, you will be able to
✓ identify the existence and power of controlling factors in a system.
✓ calculate combinations of factors.
✓ explain how adding factors increases a system's complexity.

Equipment

calculator

Figure 1 A restaurant is a surprisingly complex system.

Procedure

- You've decided to open a pizza parlor that offers the best pizza in town. Since you're new to the business, you don't want things to be too complicated. You decide to offer the following menu.

Sizes	Toppings
small	sausage
medium	pepperoni
large	extra cheese

- A customer orders a basic cheese pizza in the size of his choice. He then adds as many extra toppings as he wants at $0.50 each.

1. Including the basic cheese pizza (no toppings), how many pizza-topping combinations are possible? List them!

_____

_____

_____

2. How many different pizzas are possible? Explain.

_____

• Your best friend visits your pizza parlor and complains that you don't offer pineapple on your topping list. You add pineapple to the list to make him happy.

3. How many topping combinations are now possible?

_____

4. How many different pizzas are possible?

_____

5. What appears to happen to the possible number of topping combinations when you add just one more topping choice?

_____

• Your business is doing well, but a lot of people ask you to offer a "personal" pizza for lunch. You agree that it's a good idea and add a fourth size to your menu, which now looks like this.

Sizes	Toppings
personal	sausage
small	pepperoni
medium	extra cheese
large	pineapple

6. How many different pizzas are possible?

_____

7. Adding a topping and adding a size didn't change the total possible number of pizzas in the same way. Why not?

_____

_____

_____

• You're doing so well that you hire another pizza chef. She happens to know a great recipe for thin crust. You decide to offer both thick and thin crust pizzas.

8. How many crust and size combinations are there now? List them.

_____

_____

_____

9. How many pizzas are now possible?

_____

- People love your pizza, but they keep asking for more toppings. You introduce a new menu.

name_____

Size	Crust	Toppings
personal	thick	sausage
small	thin	pepperoni
medium		extra cheese
large		pineapple
		anchovies
		ham
		green peppers
		onions
		jalapeños
		bacon

10. How many topping combinations are possible now?

_____

11. How many pizzas are possible?

_____

As you can see, your world got very complicated very quickly!

Scientists call a world like your pizza parlor a *system*. The individual things that control how the system behaves are called *factors*. Each factor can have a certain number of possible *values*.

12. How many factors does your pizza parlor system have? List each factor. How many values are possible for each factor? Indicate the number in parentheses after each factor.

_____

_____

Just a few factors give you a huge number of pizza possibilities. If you had to list every possible pizza, you would be working very late! What would happen if you started adding other factors, like drinks, breadsticks, sauces, combo offers, and so on? The total number of choices would quickly become almost impossible to work out.

Scientists face this problem every day when they try to model complicated systems. The forces on a flying airplane, the millisecond-by-millisecond expansion of an explosion, and the weather are all systems with many factors. Constructing models of any of them is far from easy.

Consider something as simple as a tic-tac-toe game. How many possible games can there be? You might be surprised to learn that there are about 26,000. More complicated games like chess have so many possible combinations that even the best chess software can explore only a tiny number of them.

13. How do you think scientists build workable models of highly complicated systems?

_____

_____

_____

14. Are these models still useful? Explain.

_____

_____

_____

15. Do scientists need to be careful when they draw conclusions from these models? Explain.

_____

_____

_____

16. Will we ever be able to totally model something as complex as the weather? Why or why not?

_____

_____

_____

Courtesy of RIKEN

Figure 2 As of November 2011, the Fujitsu K supercomputer was the fastest computer in the world. It could perform 10.51 quadrillion calculations per second! Supercomputers play a major role in climate modeling.

21B Models that Mislead

Scientists spend a lot of time making models. As you've learned, models are not necessarily miniature objects. In fact, most scientific models are made from numbers. You've already made a few models yourself. Scientists create models as attempts to describe some part of the physical world. The better the model is, the better it works.

Scientists often use models to predict the behavior of something. For example, when you see a meteorologist forecasting next week's weather, you're seeing a model at work. Weather scientists create giant mathematical models to describe the factors that shape weather. Then they use the model to predict what's going to happen in the near future.

But models have limitations. All are simplified to some degree. And scientists often have to work with limited data. The less data they have, the weaker the model will be. So scientists must recognize their models' weaknesses. More importantly, they have to realize that a model's predictions might be wrong because of some factor that they didn't consider or understand. In this lab, we're going to build a model of something that's probably very important to you right now: growth. And we're going to test the model's predictive power. You may be surprised where it leads!

Procedure 1 (Extrapolated Model)

- Pediatricians know that a child's growth indicates his or her overall health. A child who is growing too quickly or too slowly may have a serious health problem. But how does a doctor know what's "correct"? He needs a model of typical human growth. Let's imagine that we're building this kind of model.

- You've gone to a local elementary school and measured several hundred children ranging from 5 to 12 years old. You've averaged the data and created a table of "typical" heights for each age. You've also divided the data by gender. After all, boys and girls may grow differently. The table on the next page shows your results.

name_____

section_____   date_____

Goals

After completing this lab, you will be able to
✓ identify the limitations of scientific models.
✓ construct a model from a collection of data.
✓ list ways that models can mislead.
✓ apply model limitations to the subject of climate change.

Equipment

graph paper (provided)
ruler
colored pens or pencils

Figure 1 A child's growth reflects his or her overall health.

Age (yrs.)	Male Height (cm)	Female Height (cm)
5	109	108
5.5	112	111
6	115	115
6.5	119	118
7	122	121
7.5	125	125
8	128	128
8.5	131	130
9	134	133
9.5	136	135
10	139	138
10.5	141	141
11	144	144
11.5	146	148
12	149	151

derived from http://www.cdc.gov/growthcharts

- Using the graphing area on page 196, create two separate graphs, one for males and one for females. The *x*-axis represents age. The *y*-axis represents height. Draw a smooth curve between the points.

- Your graphs model human growth from the ages of 5 to 12. If your data is good, the models should correctly describe this age group. Look at the curves and note their shapes. Also, notice the curves' overall trends. Remember, the term *trend* refers to the way the graph behaves.

1. According to the model, is there any significant difference between male and female growth? How do you know?

_____

_____

2. Does human growth appear to be fairly constant? How do you know?

_____

_____

3. Based on your model, approximately how many centimeters per year does a child typically grow?

_____

4. According to the model, approximately how tall should a typical person be at 10 years 8 months?

_____

- In order to work out the answer to the previous question, you had to estimate the value between two data points. This process is called *interpolation*. Now let's use our models to make some predictions both backward and forward in time. We didn't collect actual data for ages younger than 5 or older than 12. So we need to "extend" the curves. Scientists call this tactic *extrapolation*.

- Using a different colored pencil, extend the curves back to age 0 and forward to age 20. To draw the extension back to 0, place the ruler on the three data points at the beginning of the plot (ages 5, 5.5, and 6). Then draw a line along the ruler back to 0. Extend the other end of the curve to 20 using the same technique. The goal is to make the extensions look like a natural continuation of the curve.

- In theory, our models can now predict height at ages from 0 through 20 years.

5. According to the model, is there any significant difference between male and female growth between ages 0 and 5? Explain.

_____

_____

6. According to the extrapolated model, how tall is an average child at age 2? at birth?

name _____

_____

7. Does the birth height seem realistic? Explain.

_____

_____

8. According to the extrapolated model, is there any significant difference between male and female growth between ages 12 and 20? Explain.

_____

_____

9. According to the extrapolated model, how tall is an average male at 20? an average female?

_____

10. Do these heights seem realistic? Why or why not?

_____

_____

11. What is another problem with the extrapolated 12 to 20 year part of the model? (*Hint*: Think about a person's height at age 50.)

_____

_____

_____

12. Our models work fine between ages 5 and 12 but fail at earlier and later ages. What can we do to improve the model?

_____

Procedure 2 (Real Data Model)

- Let's add some real data and see how it compares to our extrapolated curves. The table on the next page contains average height data for ages 0 to 4.5 years and 12.5 to 20 years.

- Add this data to your graphs. Draw a smooth curve between the points using the original pencil color.

1. Based on the real data, is there any significant difference between male and female growth between ages 0 and 5? If there is, describe it.

_____

_____

Age (years)	Male Height (cm)	Female Height (cm)
0	50	49
0.5	67	65
1	76	74
1.5	82	80
2	87	86
2.5	92	91
3	96	95
3.5	99	97
4	102	101
4.5	106	104
12.5	152	155
13	156	157
13.5	160	159
14	164	160
14.5	167	161
15	170	162
15.5	172	162
16	174	163
16.5	175	163
17	175	163
17.5	176	163
18	176	163
18.5	176	163
19	177	163
19.5	177	163
20	177	163

derived from http://www.cdc.gov/growthcharts

2. Based on the real data, is there any significant difference between male and female growth between ages 12 and 20? If there is, describe it.

_____

_____

3. Based on the real data, how tall is a typical child at age 2? at birth?

_____

4. Based on the real data, how tall is an average male at 20? an average female?

_____

5. At what age has the average male essentially finished growing? the average female?

_____

- Let's compare the real data and the extrapolated data models.
6. Look at the extrapolated curve from 0 to 5 years. At what point does the extrapolated curve cease to match the real data?

_____

_____

7. Look at the extrapolated curve from 12 to 20 years. At what point does the extrapolated curve cease to match the real data?

_____

_____

- We've seen how models can mislead us when we extrapolate beyond our data. Let's consider what we can learn from this exercise.
8. What can we do to make a model approximate reality as closely as possible?

_____

_____

9. Is extrapolation worthless since it can produce misleading models? Explain.

_____

_____

_____

10. What does the difference between the male and female models after age 12 demonstrate to us?

name _____

_____

_____

_____

Modeling lies at the heart of the climate-change debate that's occupying scientists and politicians worldwide. Many scientists believe that the earth will grow significantly warmer in the next few decades, causing many serious problems. They believe that human activity causes much of this warming. These beliefs are based, in part, on large numerical models of the earth's climate.

As a result of the models' predictions, some politicians have proposed aggressive policy changes to slow or halt climate change. However, many of these proposals would significantly lower the quality of human life. Some are based on the idea that there are too many humans on the earth.

Regrettably, many people, politicians included, are not aware that climate-change models have limitations. Scientists have been modeling the earth's climate for only about 50 years. They have actual weather data for just a few hundred years. And some of that data is inferred from other measurements, not measured directly. Consequently, we just don't know how good our models really are.

As you discovered with your extrapolated growth curves, making future predictions from extrapolation can be misleading. Similarly, predicting future world temperatures by the same method could also be misleading. At this point, we just can't be confident in our models since we don't have enough data. We also don't have enough experience in understanding the complexity of the earth's climate. While our weekly weather predictions work well, long-range extrapolation is much trickier.

11. Since our climate models are limited, how far should policy-makers go in trying to control the earth's climate? Write a short paragraph answering this question. Be sure to use the Christian worldview as the basis for your responses!

_____

_____

_____

_____

Human Growth (male)

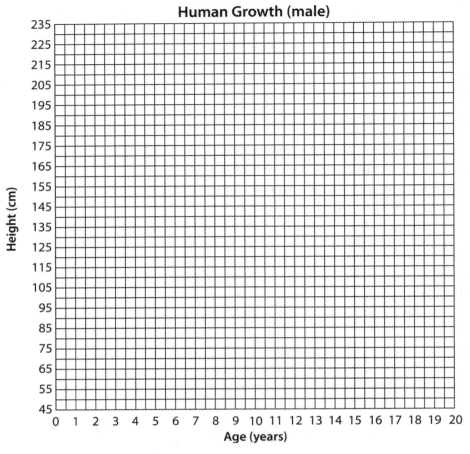

Age (years)

Human Growth (female)

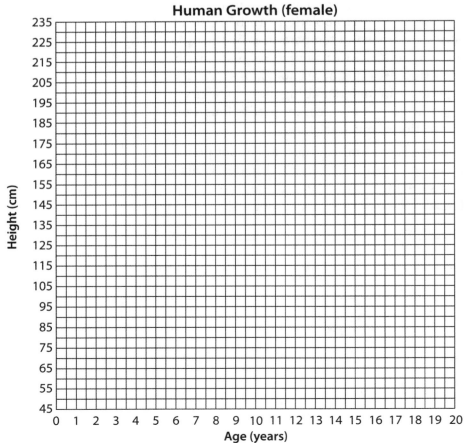

Age (years)

22 THE SUN, MOON, AND EARTH SYSTEM

22A Time Exposure

How long does it take to capture a photograph? A typical camera needs between 1 and 33 milliseconds. That's not a lot of time! Usually, that's what we want, a frozen moment of time. But sometimes, we want to capture an event that happens slowly. A good example is a *solargraph*, a single, still photograph that includes the sun taken over a period of months.

The earth rotates on its axis once a day. Because of this rotation, the sun appears to move across the sky from east to west. But the earth's axis is tilted, and the earth orbits the sun once per year. This second motion, along with the tilt, causes the sun's path across the sky to move up and down.

We don't notice this second motion because it's very gradual. The sun's path rises in the sky from December 21 until June 21. It then moves down from June 21 until December 21. A solargraph shows this motion. Each day's path is a streak of light. The next day's path will be higher or lower than the previous one. Let's build a special camera so we can observe the seasonal motions of the sun.

Procedure 1 (Building the Camera)

- Drill a ⅜ in. hole through the side of the pipe halfway between the ends. Carefully remove any burrs with a sharp knife.

- Spray paint the inside of the pipe black. Also, spray the inside of all four caps. Do *not* spray the outside of any piece.

- Wait for the paint to dry. Glue a flat cap in one end of the pipe. Glue a pipe cap over the same end.

- Place the metal square on a wood scrap. Using the pin, carefully "drill" a pinhole in the middle of the square. Twirl the pin so the hole is as round as possible.

- Position the metal square over the hole in the pipe. Gently curve the metal so it matches the pipe's curve. Glue it in place. Tape the edges with black electrical tape to hold it while it dries. Leave the tape in place so light won't leak around the plate's edges.

- When everything has dried completely, place a small piece of black electrical tape over the pinhole.

- Go into a room that can be made very dark, such as an interior bathroom or a closet. Let a tiny amount of light into the room through the gap under the door. Wait a few minutes for your eyes to adjust.

- When you can see fairly well, open the envelope of photographic paper. Remove one sheet. Curve it gently and

Goals

After completing this lab, you will be able to
✓ build a solar camera.
✓ take a long-exposure solar photograph.
✓ describe solar motion based on the photograph.

Equipment

3 in. PVC pipe, 8 in. long
3 in. PVC pipe caps (2)
3 in. PVC pipe flat caps (2)
drill and ⅜ in. drill bit
utility knife
flat black spray paint
1×1 in. thin metal square
pin or thin sewing needle
all-purpose plastic cement
black electrical tape
5×7 in. B&W photographic paper
computer with scanner and graphics program

Caution!

Be sure to wear old clothes when using spray paint. Spray painting should be done outside to avoid spraying furniture, walls, or the floor.

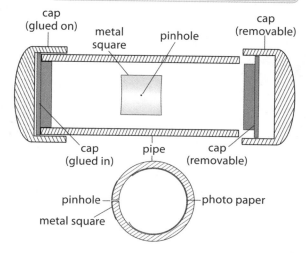

Figure 1 Solar camera design

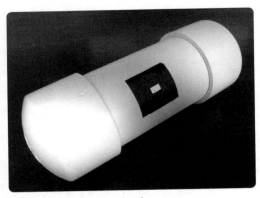

Figure 2 Completed solar camera

Figure 3 Typical solargraph

insert it into the pipe with the shiny side facing the pinhole. Position the paper so that the hole is directly over the center of the sheet.

- Insert the second flat cap into the open end of the pipe. Place the remaining pipe cap over the end. Wrap a piece of black electrical tape around the cap to keep it from coming off.

- Before opening the door, make sure the envelope of photographic paper is sealed to prevent exposing it to light.

Procedure 2 (Making a Solargraph)

- Find a location that faces either east or west and has a clear view of the sky. Fasten the camera to a sturdy object that can't move. The camera may be vertical or horizontal. The pinhole should face the horizon.

- Carefully remove the piece of electrical tape covering the pinhole. Record the date. Your solar photography experiment has begun!

- Leave the camera undisturbed for one to six months.

- When you're finished taking the picture, place a piece of black tape over the pinhole. Remove the camera and take it home. Record the date.

- Turn off all the lights around your computer. Use the light from the screen to see. Start your scanner and its software.

- Uncap the pipe and remove the photographic paper. Place it shiny-side down on the scanner.

- Scan the paper quickly using full color mode and a resolution between 200 and 300 dpi (dots per inch).

- Once you've scanned and saved the image, you may turn on the lights.

- Take a look at the photographic paper. It will darken fairly soon, so examine the image right away.

1. What do you notice about the image compared to the original scene?

_____

_____

_____

- Using a graphics program, invert the digital image so it looks "normal." This function is usually called **Invert**. For example, if you're using Adobe Photoshop,™ select **Image | Adjustments | Invert**. The picture is now a positive image.

- Print the picture using a color printer.

2. If you started a solargraph on June 21 and ended on August 1, how would you know which streak is the first and which is the last? Explain.

name _____

_____

_____

_____

3. If you started a solargraph on June 6 and ended on July 6, how would you know which streak is the first and which is the last? Explain.

_____

_____

_____

4. Look at the solargraph in the margin. Assuming it was started on April 20 and ended on August 8, approximately where are the streaks for those days? Explain.

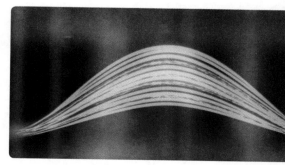

_____

_____

_____

5. The August 8 streak overlaps an earlier one. What is the approximate date of the earlier streak? Explain.

Figure 4 Example solargraph

_____

_____

_____

• Based on what you now know, label the beginning and ending streaks on your own solargraph.

6. Why are the streaks curved rather than flat?

_____

_____

7. The streaks seem almost too curved. Do you have any idea why?

_____

_____

_____

8. Some streaks may look like dashed lines instead of smooth lines. Some entire days may be "missing." Explain these.

_____

_____

_____

22B The Giant Clock

Can you tell time without a clock? We're so used to looking at our watches, computers, and phones that we don't think about other ways to tell time. Throughout most of history, however, people didn't have mechanical or electronic timekeepers. How did they manage? Genesis 1:14 tells us that God put clocks in the sky at the very beginning.

After the Flood, humans quickly relearned how to use the sun to tell time. They realized that the sun moves across the sky every day at a predictable rate. Eventually, they constructed devices that would help them tell time using the sun. These devices, called *sundials*, read the giant clock in the sky and helped them plan their days. Let's learn a bit about sundials by building one and using it to tell time.

Procedure 1 (Building the Sundial)

Sundials work by using the sun to cast a shadow on a flat plate. The shadow-casting device, called a *gnomon* (NO mon), is often just a right triangle mounted on the plate. As the earth turns, the shadow moves in response to the sun's apparent motion. Lines on the plate, known as *hour lines*, tell the time.

To tell accurate time, the sundial must be designed for the latitude of the place where it will be used. The gnomon must be tilted in relation to the latitude. The hour lines must also be drawn at angles based upon the latitude.

- Look up your latitude using a map, GPS, or online map resource. Round it to the nearest degree and record it below.

_____

- Take the sheet of paper and draw a straight line with a ruler down the middle of the wide side. Write the letter *N* at the top and the letter *S* at the bottom. We'll call this line the *N-S line*.

- Measure up 2 cm from the bottom edge of the paper and put a mark on the N-S line. Draw a 20 cm line on each side of the N-S line. Be sure the lines are perpendicular to the N-S line (use the protractor).

- Place the protractor's index hole at the intersection of the three lines. The N-S line should pass through the 90° mark at the top of the protractor. Your teacher will give you a chart with the correct angles for each hour line. Mark these angles carefully.

- Remove the protractor and draw 20 cm lines from the intersection of the three lines through the angle marks. Starting on the left side of the page, label the lines with the times listed on the chart. The first line is 6:00, the second 6:30, and so on. The N-S line should be labeled 12:00. Glue the paper to a matching sheet of foamcore when you're finished.

name_____

section_____   date_____

Goals

After completing this lab, you will be able to
- ✓ explain how solar timekeeping works.
- ✓ build a sundial.
- ✓ calculate corrections to fix the difference between solar and clock time.

Equipment

protractor
metal centimeter ruler
utility knife
foamcore sheet (¼ in.), 24×24 in. or larger
large sheet of paper, 11×17 in.
glue stick
hot glue gun and sticks
magnetic compass

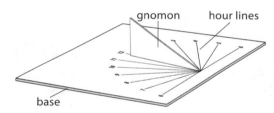

Figure 1 A typical sundial

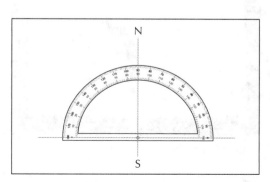

Figure 2 Drawing the hour lines

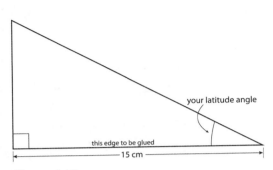

Figure 3 The gnomon

Figure 4 The sundial aligned to *geographic* north. The declination is 6°W in this case.

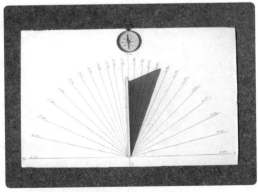

Figure 5 Reading the sundial (14:10 or 2:10 PM)

- Draw a 15 cm line on a foamcore scrap. Using the protractor, draw a second line at an angle equal to your latitude. Draw a third line at a right angle to the 15 cm line so that you end up with a right triangle. Using the utility knife and the ruler, carefully cut out the triangle. This piece is the sundial's gnomon. Be sure not to cut the table or yourself!

- Put a bead of hot glue on the 15 cm edge of the gnomon. Glue it to the sundial base so that the triangle's point is on the intersection of the hour lines (see Figure 1). Center the gnomon on the N-S line. Be sure the gnomon is standing perpendicular to the base. When the glue has cooled, put a bead of hot glue down each side of the gnomon to make it stronger.

Procedure 2 (Telling Time)

For your sundial to work correctly, it must be aligned with the N-S line pointing to the *geographic* North Pole. But a compass points to the *magnetic* North Pole. To align your sundial correctly you must know how different magnetic north is from geographic north in your part of the world. This difference is called *magnetic declination*.

- Your teacher will either tell you your declination or direct you to a website that provides this information. Declination is measured in degrees and will be either east (positive) or west (negative). Round your declination to the nearest degree and record it below. Be sure to include *E* or *W* as well!

_____

- Go outside to a sunny place. Put the sundial on a level spot or table. Place the compass on the N-S line with N at the top and S at the bottom. In other words, the N-S line on the sundial should pass through the compass card's N and S marks.

- Slowly rotate the *sundial* until the compass needle lines up along the sundial's N-S line. The sundial is now pointing to *magnetic* north.

- If your declination is west, turn the sundial *clockwise* until the compass needle is over the compass card degree mark equal to your declination value. If your declination is east, turn the sundial *counterclockwise* the correct number of degrees. Now the sundial is pointing to *geographic* north and will tell accurate time.

- Once you have the sundial properly aligned, tape or weight it in place so it won't move.

- Locate the shadow and identify the hour line that it's resting on. If it's between lines, estimate the time to the nearest 10 minutes.

• Record the sundial time in the table below. Also record the clock time. Over the next few hours, repeat this step to fill in the table.

name _____

Sundial Time	Clock Time	Corrected Time

1. Do the sundial and clock times match?

_____

Clock time and sundial times may not match for a number of reasons. In order to tell clock time with a sundial, you must add or subtract minutes to the sundial time, depending on several factors. Doing this is called *correcting* the sundial.

If you are currently on daylight savings time (DST), you need to add 60 minutes to the sundial time. DST starts in the spring and ends in the autumn. However, not all parts of the world use DST. Ask your teacher if you're not sure.

• Record your daylight savings correction below (+60 minutes if you are on DST, +0 minutes if you're not).

_____

Clock time is also based on your *time zone*. Time zones were created in the nineteenth century so that railroads could have standard schedules. While all clocks within a time zone show the same time, the zone is wide enough that the sun is in different places depending upon where you are located.

Clock time equals the sun time at the *middle* of the time zone. If you are east or west of the middle, you need to add or subtract time.

• Your teacher will tell you the longitude of the middle of your time zone. Record this value below.

_____

• Look up your location's longitude using a map, GPS, or online resource. Round it to the nearest degree and record it below.

_____

• Subtract the time zone longitude value from your location's longitude. Record the result below. Be sure to include the + or – sign!

_____

- Multiply the result by 4 minutes. This result equals the longitude correction. Record it below. Be sure to include the + or – sign!

  _____

- Add the daylight savings time correction and the longitude correction. Record the result below.

  _____

- This number represents the amount of time you must add to your sundial time to make it equal clock time. Add the correction to each of the sundial times in the table on the previous page and record the corrected times in the **Corrected Time** column. Compare the corrected times to the clock times.

2. Do the corrected sundial and clock times match more closely now?

   _____

3. Ideally, your corrected sundial time should perfectly match clock time. List factors that could keep them from matching perfectly.

   _____

   _____

   _____

4. Sundials are often sold as garden ornaments. Why will they usually not be as accurate as yours?

   _____

   _____

   _____

5. Why is a mechanical or electronic clock preferable to a sundial?

   _____

   _____

   _____

22C Mastering the Moon

name_____

section_____   date_____

Everyone notices the moon, but very few people can explain its behavior. In fact, some people are surprised that they can see the moon during the daytime. After all, isn't the moon a nighttime object?

Understanding the moon's phases and its position in the sky has interested humans since the beginning of history. By the middle of the twentieth century, scientists understood the science of the moon well enough to send a spacecraft from the earth to a specific landing site on the moon.

One of the reasons that the moon is so challenging to model is due to the fact that everything is moving! The moon orbits the earth, the earth orbits the sun, and the earth rotates on its axis. It's enough to make you dizzy! In this lab, you're going to explore the sun, moon, and earth system by building a simple model. This model will make it clear why the moon shows phases. And you'll also see why the moon is visible at many different times, including the middle of the day!

Goals

After completing this lab, you will be able to
- ✓ model the sun, moon, and earth system.
- ✓ explain why the moon shows phases.
- ✓ demonstrate the link between lunar phase and the time of day the moon is visible.

Equipment

3×5 in. index cards (8)
protractor
meter stick
masking tape
volleyball
large flashlight or portable utility light

Procedure

- Clear an open space on the floor several meters across and place an *X* in the center with masking tape.

- Place the 0 end of the meter stick at the center of the *X*.

- Place two pieces of masking tape on the floor, one at 33 cm and one at 1 m.

- Using the protractor, rotate the meter stick around the *X* 45° at a time and place two more tape markers on the floor at 33 cm and 1 m. Keep rotating until you have a total of 8 pairs of tape markers. The pieces of tape at 33 cm represent the earth's daily rotation. The pieces of tape at 1 m represent the moon's orbit around the earth.

- Using the index cards, create time labels. Label them as follows: **12:00 midnight**, **3:00 AM**, **6:00 AM**, **9:00 AM**, **12:00 noon**, **3:00 PM**, **6:00 PM**, and **9:00 PM**.

- Tape the cards to the floor in between the 33 cm and 1 m tape markers. Check the diagram in the margin to be sure that you've set up everything correctly. If you live in the Southern Hemisphere, place 12:00 noon at the same place, but reverse the order of the other cards.

- You will need three people to complete the sun, moon, and earth model. One will hold the light (the sun), one will hold the volleyball (the moon), and one will stand inside and observe (the earth).

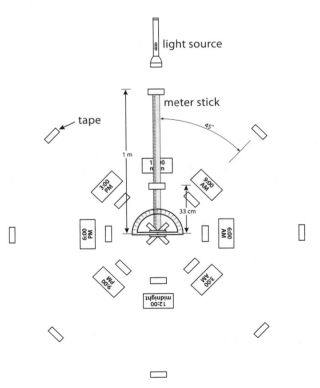

Figure 1 Arrangement of floor marks and labels for completing the lab

Figure 2 Modeling the sun, moon, and earth system

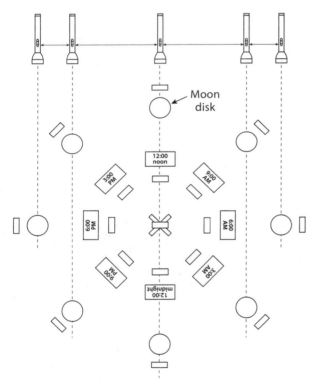

Figure 3 Adjusting the sun's position

- The person acting as the sun should stand 1 m away from the 12:00 noon 1 m tape marker and hold the light pointing straight ahead toward the earth.

- The person acting as the moon should stand with the volleyball held above the 12:00 noon 1 m tape marker.

- The person acting as the earth should stand on the 12:00 noon 33 cm tape marker. The person acting as the moon should hold the ball at the earth's eye level. You may need to turn off the room lights to see the shadowed and lighted portions of the moon more clearly.

- The earth should look at the moon and draw what he sees in the **Phase** column of the table on the next page. Look at the moon itself, not the sun. Shade in any part of the circle that looks dark. Leave any lit part of the circle unshaded.

- After recording the moon's phase, the earth should hold both of his arms straight out from his sides. They will represent the horizon. If you live in the Northern Hemisphere, his left hand is the eastern horizon, and his right hand is the western horizon. If you live in the Southern Hemisphere, his left hand is the western horizon, and his right hand is the eastern horizon.

  - The earth should step to the 3:00 PM tape marker, making sure he continues facing outward. If the moon is in front of his extended arms, it's above the horizon and therefore visible. If it's behind his arms, it's below the horizon and not visible.

  - The earth should go around the circle from marker to marker and determine when the moon first rises (comes in front of his arms) and when it sets (goes behind his arms). Record these times in the table on the next page.

  - When the earth has come back to the 12:00 noon marker, the moon should move counterclockwise to the next tape marker. This position represents a change of about 3½ days of the lunar cycle.

  - In order to simulate the nearly parallel rays of the sun, the light must move for each new moon position. However, the sun should *not* move in a circle. Instead, he should move in a line. The diagram in the margin shows the correct sun position for each new moon position.

  - Record the new phase and then work out the moon's rising and setting times. Repeat these steps until you've done all eight positions of the moon.

Phase	Time Moon Rises	Time Moon Sets
◯		
◯		
◯		
◯		
◯		
◯		
◯		
◯		

name _____

1. How many hours is the moon above the horizon each day?

    _____

2. At what time will the full moon be highest in the sky? Explain.

    _____

    _____

    _____

3. Why does a new moon happen?

    _____

    _____

    _____

4. What is the relationship of the sun, moon, and earth when we see a full moon? Why does this relationship give a full moon?

    _____

    _____

    _____

5. Explain what causes the moon's phases. Be specific!

_____

_____

_____

6. During which phase is a lunar eclipse possible? Explain why.

_____

_____

_____

7. During which phase is a solar eclipse possible? Explain why.

_____

_____

_____

8. Understanding the moon's behavior is interesting. But does it have any practical value? Explain why or why not.

_____

_____

_____

_____

_____

23 OUR SOLAR SYSTEM

23A Being a Galileo

name_____

section_____ date_____

Have you ever wondered what it's like to make a really big scientific discovery? We're so used to science that it's hard to imagine the sense of wonder early scientists must have experienced. Picture how Galileo felt when he first looked at the night sky through his telescope.

We know what happened because Galileo described his findings in a book. Called *Sidereus Nuncius* ("Starry Messenger"), Galileo's book reports three key discoveries. He saw mountains on the moon, far more stars than could be seen by the eye alone, and four strange objects near Jupiter.

The last discovery was the most important. Galileo quickly realized that the four objects must be moving because they changed position each night. Galileo's notes of his observations looked something like this:

```
*    *    O    *

     O    *    *    *

*    *    O

*    *    O

*    *    O    *

*         O    *    *    *

          O    *    *    *    *
```

Today we're used to the idea of satellite bodies orbiting a planet. But in Galileo's time, this idea was totally new. It helped change scientists' ideas about the solar system. It also showed how useful the telescope could be. In this lab, you're going to be a Galileo for a few nights.

Procedure

- Your teacher will tell you when and where Jupiter will be visible during the evening. Jupiter looks like a very bright star. If you have good eyesight and it's very dark, it can look like a tiny disk.

- Look at Jupiter with a telescope or a pair of binoculars. Draw what you see in the table on the next page. Use Galileo's style: O for Jupiter and * for the moons. Try to draw the distances between the objects as accurately as possible.

- Repeat your observations for at least four more nights. Depending on the weather, it may take you a week or two to complete your observations.

Goals

After completing this lab, you will be able to
✓ repeat Galileo's Jupiter observations.
✓ draw conclusions about the Galilean moons of Jupiter.

Equipment

small telescope or binoculars

Figure 1 Galileo's discovery of four moons orbiting Jupiter had a major impact on the future of astronomy.

Date and Time	Observation

1. What is the maximum number of moons you saw?

_____

2. How were you able to tell the difference between a moon and a nearby star?

_____

_____

3. Why do you think some moons disappear on certain nights?

_____

_____

4. Do the four moons orbit in the same plane? Or does each moon orbit Jupiter in its own plane? How do you know?

_____

_____

5. On some nights, a moon appears more like a blob of light than a point. What do you think you're seeing?

_____

_____

_____

6. Why is direct observation still important today? Wouldn't looking up Jupiter's moons on the Internet be just as useful as seeing them with a real telescope?

_____

_____

_____

Optional Activity

- Look up the names of the four moons. Also look up the position of their orbits. See if you can label the moons in your observations.

23B Elliptical Excursions

If you had been an astronomer living during the years 1600–1610, you would have lived an exciting life. Galileo introduced the telescope as an astronomical instrument. His discoveries included moons orbiting Jupiter, mountains on Earth's moon, and many stars that couldn't be seen with the eye alone but that gave the Milky Way its glow. A spectacular supernova appeared in 1604. Everyone was arguing about the geocentric and heliocentric theories. And in 1609 Johannes Kepler published his first two laws of planetary motion in a book called *Astronomia nova* ("A New Astronomy").

Kepler's laws became the basis of modern mathematical astronomy. Isaac Newton later expanded and improved Kepler's work as a part of his own studies on the laws of motion.

Kepler's first law of planetary motion states that planets move in elliptical orbits with the sun at one focus. An *ellipse* is the shape formed by cutting a closed slice out of a cone. It often looks similar to a flattened circle. In math, an ellipse is defined as the path of a point moving around two fixed points called *foci*. Let's learn about ellipses by drawing and measuring a few.

Procedure

- Divide a sheet of paper into four equal parts by drawing two perpendicular lines down the middle of each side.

- Mark two dots on the longer line 2 cm on each side of the intersection of the two lines. These points are going to be the ellipse's foci. The distance between the foci is therefore 4 cm.

- Tape the paper to the sheet of cardboard. Insert a pushpin into each focus.

- Tie the string into a loop. Place the loop over the pushpins.

- Place the pencil point inside the string at the knot.

- Pull the string tight, place the pencil point on the paper with the pencil held vertically, and begin tracing out the ellipse. Keep the string tight at all times!

- After completing the drawing, measure to the nearest 0.1 cm the length of the ellipse along the longer line. This length is called the *major axis*. Record it in the table on the next page.

- Measure to the nearest 0.1 cm the length of the ellipse along the shorter line. This length is called the *minor axis*. Record it in the table.

- Draw two more ellipses on separate sheets of paper. The first one should have foci 6 cm apart. The second should have foci 8 cm apart. Perform the same measurements and record them in the table.

name_____

section_____ date_____

Goals

After completing this lab, you will be able to
- ✓ define the terms describing an ellipse.
- ✓ draw an ellipse.
- ✓ explain the significance of the ellipse in Kepler's first law.

Equipment

sheet of corrugated cardboard,
    12×12 in. or larger
sheets of paper (3)
thin string, 25 cm
centimeter ruler
mechanical pencil
masking tape
pushpins (2)
calculator

Figure 1 Kepler's book *Astronomia nova* introduced two of his three planetary laws.

Figure 2 Drawing the ellipse

Cone Cutting

The ellipse is one of three geometric figures produced by cutting a cone with a plane. These figures are known as *conic sections*. The three conic sections are the *ellipse*, the *parabola*, and the *hyperbola*.

Although several ancient mathematicians explored conic sections, it was Apollonius of Perga (c. 262 – c. 190 BC) who gave them the names we still use today.

All three are important in astronomy and space science. You'll learn more about them in later math courses.

1. Look carefully at your three ellipses. Is there a relationship to the distance between the foci and the shape of the ellipse? Explain.

2. If you moved the foci very close together, what shape would the ellipse resemble?

Mathematicians use a number to describe an ellipse's shape. This number is called the ellipse's *eccentricity*. It's calculated with the following formula:

$$\text{eccentricity} = \frac{\text{foci distance (cm)}}{\text{major axis (cm)}}.$$

- Calculate the eccentricity of each of your ellipses. Round the result to two decimal places and record it in the table below.

Ellipse	Foci Distance (cm)	Major Axis (cm)	Minor Axis (cm)	Eccentricity
1	4			
2	6			
3	8			

3. Describe the relationship between the eccentricity of the ellipse and its shape.

4. If an ellipse has an eccentricity of 0, what shape is it?

5. How far apart will the foci be if an ellipse has an eccentricity of 0?

According to Kepler's first law, all the planets orbit the sun in elliptical paths. Yet everyone before Kepler thought the planets had to move in circular paths. Why did they miss the ellipse as the correct shape? Take a look at the table on the next page. It shows the eccentricity of each of the planets that people could see without a telescope. Earth is also included on the list.

Planet	Orbital Eccentricity
Mercury	0.21
Venus	0.01
Earth	0.02
Mars	0.09
Jupiter	0.05
Saturn	0.06

name_____

6. Based on the table, why do you think everyone before Kepler thought the planets moved in circular orbits?

_____

_____

7. Based on what you learned in your textbook, what enabled Kepler to realize that the planets' orbits were actually ellipses rather than circles?

_____

_____

_____

8. Kepler discovered his first law when he was trying to determine Mars's orbit. If he had been studying Venus instead, is it likely that he would have discovered the true shape of planetary orbits? Explain why or why not.

_____

_____

_____

• Mark two points anywhere along the path of your first ellipse. Label them *A* and *B*. Measure the distances from *A* to each focus and record them in the table below. Add these two measurements and record the sum in the table. Now measure and record the distances from each focus to *B*. Add these measurements and record the sum in the table.

Point	Distance to Focus 1 (cm)	Distance to Focus 2 (cm)	Sum (cm)
A			
B			

9. Are the two sums similar?

_____

10. Kepler and others spent many years of their lives trying to work out the details of planetary motion. To some people, this may seem like a waste of time about a relatively trivial and impractical matter. In a few sentences, explain the value of work like Kepler's.

_____

_____

_____

_____

_____

23C Running Backward

name_____

section_____ date_____

Imagine you are an astronomer back in the days of ancient Greece. Temporarily forget everything you've learned about the solar system from your textbook. All you have are your eyes to observe the skies. Happily, there is almost no light pollution, so you can see things really well!

Every night you watch the planet Mars, a small reddish dot. You don't know that it's a nearby world. To you, it's a strange star that doesn't act like the others. Even though the stars move across the sky from night to night, they don't move with respect to each other. That's why people can learn to recognize constellations!

But Mars and a few other "stars" don't follow this rule. They change position compared to the other stars every night. That's why some of your fellow astronomers have named them *planets*, which means "wanderer" in Greek.

Mars does something really strange. Most of the time, it moves gradually from west to east among the fixed stars in the night sky. But every now and then it does something weird. It stops and changes direction, moving "backward" for a while. Then it stops again and starts moving forward. You can't explain this behavior.

Fast-forward to the present and restore your knowledge of the solar system (your teacher is relieved!). Let's take a look at this problem, known as *retrograde motion*.

Procedure

- Look at the diagram on page 218, which shows the orbits of Earth and Mars. Notice that both planets revolve counter-clockwise around the sun (as do all the planets). The lettered positions along each planet's orbit represent the planets' positions at the same time. The letters are one month apart.

- Using the ruler, draw a line to connect the two *A* planet positions. Then connect all the other positions in the same way. These lines represent the view from an observer on Earth watching Mars move across the sky.

- Using the protractor, measure the angle formed between each line that you drew and the reference line that passes through the center of each earth circle. Record these angles in the table on page 217. The angles help us know where in Earth's sky Mars appears.

- Now, let's create a picture of what a person on Earth will see when he watches Mars. Use the second diagram (page 219) to create this view.

- Align the protractor on the reference line above the observer's head. Place the protractor's index hole at the intersection of the two lines.

Goals

After completing this lab, you will be able to

✓ explain what is meant by apparent retrograde motion.

✓ model Earth-Mars retrograde motion.

✓ discuss the complexity of relative motion and its role in historical solar system models.

Equipment

protractor
centimeter ruler

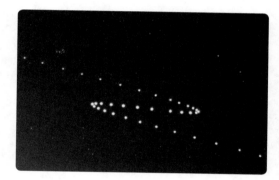

Figure 1 Mars shows very obvious retrograde motion.

Mars Madness

You may be getting the impression that only Mars shows retrograde motion. Actually, *all* the planets appear to reverse directions at times. The reason that the ancient world focused its attention on Mars was simply due to the fact that it is very visible and its retrograde motion is especially obvious. The inferior planets are visible only during a limited time (morning and evening), so their backward motion isn't very obvious. And until the development of precision astronomical instruments in the late 1500s, studying the other superior planets in detail wasn't easy.

- Make a small mark on the diagram at the same angle that you recorded for month *A*.

- Place the ruler between the center of the reference line and the mark you just made. Measure out 10 cm and draw a dot. Label it *A*.

- Repeat the previous steps for months *B* through *I*. However, reduce the measured distance by 0.1 cm each time. These distances are included in the table on page 217. Reducing the distances will help keep the dots separate.

- Draw a smooth curve from *A* to *I* in the correct alphabetical order. The line represents Mars's path across the sky over a period of months.

1. What direction across the sky does Mars move most of the time?

_____

2. What does Mars appear to do between months *D* and *F*?

_____

3. Look at the two orbits shown in the diagram on page 218. Does Mars or Earth ever change direction?

_____

4. Explain the reason for retrograde motion. (*Hint*: Examine the first diagram between months *D* and *F*.)

_____

_____

_____

Ancient astronomers believed that the earth didn't move and was the center of the solar system. So when they observed planets such as Mars apparently moving backward, they had to come up with a model that could account for this odd behavior. Look at Figure 23-2 in your textbook. Compare the loop in the planet's path to the second diagram in this lab.

5. Briefly explain the solution ancient astronomers came up with to account for this loop in a planet's path across the sky.

_____

_____

6. Today we know that this solution was incorrect. But it's still an example of a valid scientific model. Explain why.

_____

_____

_____

7. What advantage did Copernicus's heliocentric theory and Kepler's first law give to astronomers trying to explain retrograde motion? Explain.

name_____

_____

_____

_____

8. Today, astronomers call Mars's behavior *apparent retrograde motion*. Explain why they've added the word *apparent*.

_____

_____

9. Why is it understandable that astronomers took so many centuries to puzzle out things like the workings of the solar system? (*Hint*: Review the introductory paragraphs to Lab 22C.)

_____

_____

_____

10. Can we confidently claim that our current model of the solar system is completely accurate? Explain why or why not.

_____

_____

_____

Month	Angle (°)	Line Length (cm)
A		10.0
B		9.9
C		9.8
D		9.7
E		9.6
F		9.5
G		9.4
H		9.3
I		9.2

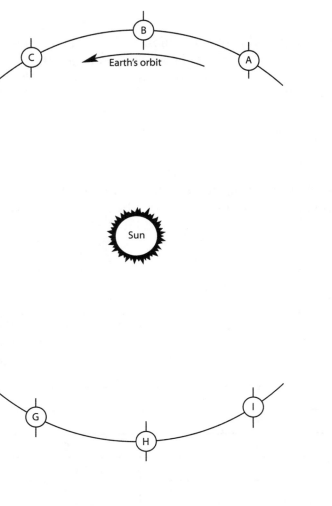

name _____

reference line

180° ———————————|——————————— 0°

24 STARS, GALAXIES, AND THE UNIVERSE

24A Sky Map

Have you ever wanted to do some stargazing but didn't know where to look? On a dark night the skies can be pretty bewildering. Locating a specific planet is harder than you'd think. Even finding the familiar constellations can be a challenge.

Of course, you could use a portable electronic device running planetarium software. But there's an easier and much simpler solution: a *constellation finder*. You can buy these from science and hobby stores. They also come with some astronomy books. In this lab, you're going to build a simple constellation finder. It's a low-tech but remarkably useful device that will be your map to the night skies.

Procedure 1 (Construction)

- Your teacher will give you two templates that make up the constellation finder. The first is called the **Frame Sheet** and is rectangular. The second one is circular and has the constellations printed on it. It's called the **Constellation Disk**. Cut out the Constellation Disk. Cut out the Frame Sheet along the thick dashed line.

- Using the glue stick, attach the Constellation Disk to a sheet of construction paper. When the glue is dry, carefully cut around the circle to remove the extra paper.

- Glue the Frame Sheet onto another piece of construction paper. When the glue is dry, trim away any excess paper.

- Carefully cut out the shaded areas of the Frame Sheet using a hobby knife, being careful not to cut into any of the borders. Do not cut the table or yourself!

- Staple the third sheet of construction paper onto the back of the Frame Sheet. Place staples at the four positions that are marked on the Frame Sheet.

- Sandwich the Constellation Disk between the Frame Sheet and the back sheet of construction paper. Align the edge of the Constellation Disk with the upper edge of the circular cutouts on the Frame Sheet so that the months and days are clearly visible in the windows.

- Use a small piece of tape to fasten the Constellation Disk in place temporarily. Don't press it down since you'll remove the tape later!

- Punch a hole through the + in the center of the Constellation Disk and also through the back sheet of construction paper.

name_____

section_____ date_____

Goals

After completing this lab, you will be able to

✓ construct a constellation finder.

✓ use the constellation finder for basic observing.

✓ identify key stars in constellations.

Equipment

constellation finder template (available on the Teacher's Toolkit CD and on the *EARTH SCIENCE* 4th Edition Resources webpage)
sheets of construction paper (3)
glue stick
tape
scissors
hobby knife
stapler
split brad fastener

Figure 1 A commercial constellation finder

- Fasten the Constellation Disk to the back sheet of construction paper with the split brad fastener.
- Remove the temporary piece of tape and spin the Constellation Disk a few times until it turns easily.

Figure 2 Using the constellation finder

Procedure 2 (Practice)

Before you go outside on a dark night, let's do some indoor practicing with the constellation finder. We'll pretend you're observing at 8:00 PM on March 15.

- Locate the time (8:00 PM in this case) on the Frame Sheet.
- Rotate the Constellation Disk until the date (March 15) is lined up with the time (8:00 PM).
- The sky arrangement at this time and date appear in the big cutout in the center of the finder.
- Face south in your classroom. Hold the constellation finder upside down over your head so that the *N* at the top of the finder is toward your back (facing north). The constellations that appear near the center of the oval cutout will appear directly overhead as you look into the sky.

1. Which constellations appear overhead at 8:00 PM on March 15?

_____

- The perimeter of the oval cutout represents the *horizon*. Constellations located here will be found near the horizon as you look for them in the sky.

2. Which constellation is located near the northern horizon?

_____

3. Which constellation appears in the south near the horizon?

_____

- A constellation will be at its *zenith* (directly overhead) when it's in line with an imaginary line between north and south on your constellation finder. It will be at the *midpoint* when it's halfway between the zenith and the horizon.

4. At what time would Cassiopeia be nearest its zenith on October 10?

_____

name_____

5. On which date would Corona Borealis be at its zenith at 10:00 PM?

_____

6. Where would you look at 9:00 PM on January 15 to find the Great Square of Pegasus? Taurus? Leo?

_____

_____

_____

7. Where would you look at 9:00 PM on September 12 to find Cassiopeia? Hercules? Cygnus?

_____

_____

_____

8. When the star Vega (in Lyra) is at the zenith on February 15, is it visible? Explain why or why not.

_____

_____

Procedure 3 (Stargazing)

- Over the next two weeks, observe constellations at least five times. Use the constellation finder to help you.

- On a separate sheet of paper, create a table to document your observations. Include columns for **Date**, **Time**, **Constellation Name**, and **Position** in the sky. Turn in your table on the date that your teacher specifies.

24B Going the Distance

name_____

section_____   date_____

If someone asked you the distance to the nearest star (Proxima Centauri), could you give an answer? If you've read your textbook, you know that the distance is 4.24 ly. But if that person asked you to *measure* the distance yourself, could you do it? How do you measure the distance to a star?

Ancient astronomers tried to measure distances to faraway objects using indirect methods similar to those that we explored in Labs 3B and 7A. They succeeded if the object wasn't too far away. For example, Aristarchus of Samos (c. 310–230 BC) successfully measured the distance to the moon.

But when Tycho Brahe tried to measure the distance to the stars, he failed. He didn't know it, but the stars were just too far away for his instruments to measure. It wasn't until 1838 that star distance measurements became possible.

So how do you measure the distance to a nearby star? One easy method uses something called *parallax*. When you look at a distant fixed object from two different positions, it appears to move. If you can measure this apparent change, some simple geometry will give you the distance. Let's do it with something not quite so far away as a star!

Procedure

- Place a star-shaped mark made from masking tape on a wall at one end of the room. The star should *not* be centered.

- Go to the other end of the room and position two desks near the side walls. Leave enough space so you can walk around the desks.

- Place a piece of masking tape on top of each desk near the outer corner and perpendicular to the back edge The outer edges of the pieces of tape define the observational *base line*.

- Measure and record to the nearest 1 cm the length of the base line (the distance between the pieces of tape).

Goals

After completing this lab, you will be able to
- ✓ measure large distances indirectly.
- ✓ explain how parallax can be used to measure astronomical distances.
- ✓ discuss the universe's size in relation to modern cosmology.

Equipment

tape measure
cardboard sheet, 12 × 12 in.
string
protractor
tables or desks (2)
masking tape
pencil
straight pins (2)

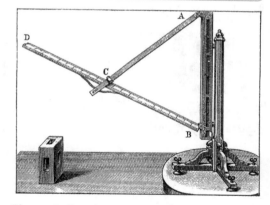

Figure 1 Renaissance astronomers used instruments like this *triquetrum* to measure parallax.

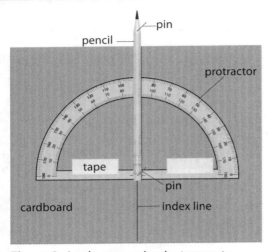

Figure 2 Angle-measuring instrument

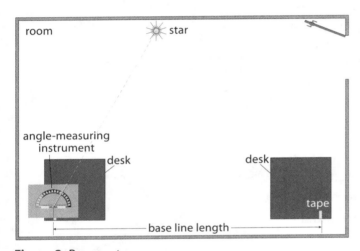

Figure 3 Room setup

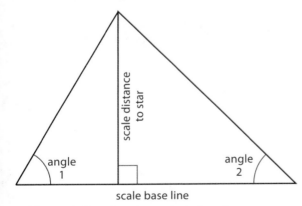

Figure 4 Creating the scaled triangle

- Place the protractor in the middle of the cardboard sheet with its straight edge parallel to the edge of the cardboard and tape it down. Draw a perpendicular index line from the protractor index hole to the parallel edge.

- Stick a pin into the pencil just behind the sharpened end. Do *not* push the pin all the way through the pencil! Stick another pin through the eraser so that the point sticks out about 7 mm. Be sure the pins are lined up with each other.

- Insert the second pin's point through the protractor's index hole and into the cardboard. You have just built an angle-measuring instrument.

- Position the rear edge of the instrument so that it is parallel with the rear edge of one of the desks and the the index mark lines up with the outer edge of the masking tape.

  - Crouch behind the desk. Look along the pencil. Without moving the protractor, rotate the pencil so that the two pins line up with the masking tape star on the wall. Record the angle to the nearest 1°. If the protractor has two scales, use the angle that's less than 90°.

  _____

  - Repeat the previous two steps at the other desk. Record the angle.

  _____

  - Now draw a scaled triangle to match the real one that you've just measured. Use a scale of 1 cm per 100 cm. Draw a base line across the bottom of the paper equal to the scaled length of the real base line. For example, if the real base line is 1000 cm long, draw a 10 cm line on the paper.

1. What is the scale of your triangle compared to the real one?

  _____

  - Remove the protractor from the cardboard. Place it on the paper with the index hole over the left end of the scaled base line. Mark the angle that you measured on the left side of the room.

  - Move the protractor to the other end of the line and mark the angle that you measured on the right side of the room.

  - Using the ruler, draw two lines from the ends of the base line through the angle marks. Extend the lines until they meet and form a triangle.

- Draw a line from the intersection of the two lines back to the base line. Be sure the ruler is perpendicular to the base line! This line represents the scaled distance to the star on the wall.

- Measure to the nearest 0.1 cm the length of the line you've just drawn and record it.

_____

2. What must you do to convert the scaled distance to the real distance?

_____

- Convert the scaled distance to the real distance and record it.

_____

- Now let's check your accuracy. Stretch a string tightly between the two tape lines on the desks. Using the tape measure, determine and record to the nearest 1 cm the distance from the star on the wall to the string. Be sure to keep the tape measure perpendicular to the wall and the string!

_____

- Calculate the percent error of your indirect measurement. If you've forgotten the equation, review Lab 2B. Round your percent error to one decimal place and record it.

_____

3. If your percent error wasn't zero, list possible reasons for the error.

_____

_____

The parallax method seems pretty simple. When it's used to measure star distances, the base line is the distance across the earth's orbit (about 300 million km). In other words, the observations are taken six months apart so the earth has time to move.

Why couldn't Tycho measure the distance to the nearest stars? Look at the diagram to the right. It shows three objects that are increasingly distant from the earth. Examine the angle formed at the point of each triangle.

4. What happens to this angle as the object gets farther and farther from the earth?

_____

name _____

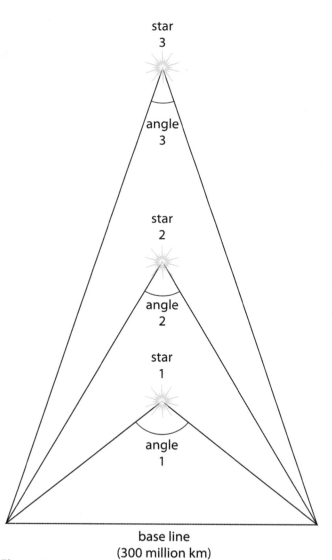

Figure 5

5. Why do you think Tycho couldn't measure the distance to the stars by the parallax method?

_____

_____

6. Even today, we cannot use parallax to measure the distance to stars farther away than 326 ly. Explain why not.

_____

_____

_____

In Tycho's time, most astronomers believed that the stars were not very far away. As time went by, astronomers realized that the stars were much more distant than they could have imagined. With Edwin Hubble's discoveries in the early twentieth century, the universe became unimaginably large.

7. Write a short essay explaining why a gigantic universe was so upsetting to people. Write a response based on the Christian worldview.

_____

_____

_____

_____

_____

_____

_____

_____

25 SPACE EXPLORATION

25A Scoping the Skies

No one is sure who invented the telescope. Hans Lipperhey, Zacharias Janssen, and Jacob Metius all claim credit. What we do know is that when Galileo pointed his telescope at the sky, everything changed. Astronomy entered a new era. The telescope was for Galileo what the space program is for us. It made the heavens reachable.

How does a telescope work? That depends on the type. A lens (refractor) telescope uses a large lens called the *objective* to gather and focus light. A second, smaller lens called the *eyepiece* magnifies the image produced by the objective. So a telescope really does two things: it gathers a lot of light and it produces a magnified image.

In this lab, you're going to build a simple *Keplerian telescope*. This type of telescope was invented by Johannes Kepler in 1611 and was a big improvement on Galileo's design. Along the way, you'll learn about how this kind of telescope works.

Procedure 1 (Measuring the Lenses)

Before we can build a telescope, we must measure each lens in a special way. By doing this, we can predict how the telescope will perform.

- Tape a sheet of white paper to a wall that is opposite a window. Turn out the room lights. Hold the "0" end of the ruler against the wall with the ruler sticking out into the room.

- Stand to one side of the ruler. Hold the objective lens from the side by its edge. Slide it along the top of the ruler while keeping it parallel to the wall. Be careful not to block the front of the lens. At some point you will see a sharp image of the scene outside the window form on the paper.

- Get the image as sharp as possible and then note the lens's position along the ruler's edge. This distance is called the lens's *focal length*. Record the distance to the nearest 1 mm.

  _____

- Repeat the previous two steps to determine the eyepiece lens's focal length. Record it below.

  _____

- Measure and record the diameter of the objective lens to the nearest 1 mm. This value is called the lens's *aperture*.

  _____

- A telescope's magnifying power can be determined with the following formula:

$$\text{magnification (power)} = \frac{\text{objective focal length (mm)}}{\text{eyepiece focal length (mm)}}.$$

Goals

After completing this lab, you will be able to
- ✓ measure lens focal length.
- ✓ calculate telescope magnification.
- ✓ construct a Keplerian telescope.
- ✓ evaluate commercial telescopes.

Equipment

paper towel tubes (2)
objective lens
eyepiece lens
centimeter ruler
masking tape
rubber band
scissors
paper

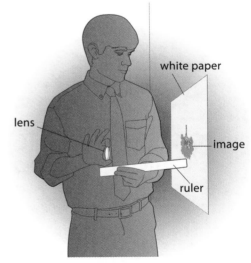

Figure 1

Focal What?

A lens's focal length is the distance between the lens and a screen when an object that is infinitely far away forms a sharp image on the screen. Obviously, the scene outside the window is not infinitely far away. But it's far enough away that it will work. A lens's focal length is one of its key optical properties. Scientists need to know this value in order to design and build instruments containing lenses.

1. You see a telescope in a department store. It has an objective focal length of 1000 mm. The eyepiece has a focal length of 4 mm. What is its magnifying power?

_____

Many people mistakenly believe that bigger is better when it comes to telescope magnification. But magnification is only part of the story. Light-gathering power is actually much more important. The objective lens's aperture determines how much light the telescope can gather.

2. One telescope has an objective lens 50 mm in diameter. Another has an objective lens 100 mm in diameter. Which gathers more light? Explain why.

_____

_____

Aperture also limits the maximum *practical magnification* a telescope can have. A small aperture means that the telescope doesn't gather enough light to magnify the image very much and still produce a sharp image. The following formula lets you calculate a telescope's practical magnification:

practical magnification (power) = aperture (mm) × 2.

3. What is the largest practical magnification of a telescope that has an objective lens 100 mm in diameter?

_____

4. You are thinking of buying that department store telescope from question 1. It has an aperture of 50 mm. Is this a good telescope? Explain why or why not.

_____

_____

_____

5. You go to a telescope store and look at a telescope with a 100 mm aperture, an objective focal length of 1000 mm, and an eyepiece focal length of 10 mm. Is this a good telescope? Explain why or why not.

_____

_____

_____

Procedure 2 (Building a Telescope)

name _____

- It's time to put our lenses together and make a telescope! If one tube slides easily into the other, skip this step. Otherwise, cut along a straight line the entire length of one side of one of the tubes. Squeeze the sides of the tube slightly until you can slide it into the other tube. Tape the tube along the cut to create a tube with a slightly smaller diameter.

- Tape the objective lens around its edges so that it is held firmly at the end of the larger tube. Make sure the lens isn't tilted in the tube.

- If your tubes fit snugly into each other, skip this step. Otherwise, make four equally spaced cuts about 2 cm long around the edge at the other end of the objective tube.

- Tape the eyepiece lens to the end of the smaller tube. Check to see that it is straight.

- Insert the smaller tube into the larger tube and slip the rubber band around the larger tube at the slits that you cut. This will hold the two tubes snug.

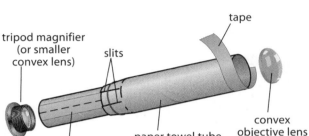

Figure 2

1. What is your telescope's theoretical magnification?

_____

2. What is your telescope's maximum practical magnification?

_____

- Point the telescope at a distant object and slide the smaller tube back and forth until the image comes into sharp focus.

3. What very obvious thing do you notice about the image?

_____

4. Look at a bright light source *other than the sun* with the telescope. What do you notice around the edges of the light source?

_____

This effect is known as *chromatic aberration*. It's caused by the glass dispersing (breaking up) white light into the colors from which it's made. The effect is similar to the way a prism disperses sunlight into a color spectrum. Early telescope makers tried to eliminate this problem and failed.

Isaac Newton built the first practical *reflector telescope* to solve this particular problem since mirrors don't break up white light like lenses do. Objective and eyepiece lenses in modern refractor telescopes are actually pairs of lenses made from two different types of glass. These reduce chromatic aberration significantly.

Not-So-Bright Ideas

Never use a telescope to observe the sun unless it's equipped with a true solar filter designed to be used on telescopes. Dark glass or plastic is not enough. Observing the sun through an unprotected telescope can damage your eyesight. Solar filters may be purchased from companies that sell telescope accessories.

Also, avoid leaving an unprotected telescope pointed at the sun for too long. A telescope can be damaged if it's overheated. Finally, a telescope can start a fire if it's pointed at the sun and the eyepiece is lined up with flammable material, such as grass.

5. On the basis of what you've just learned, explain why good-quality telescopes are not inexpensive.

_____

_____

_____

_____

_____

25B Reaction Time

name _____

section _____ date _____

Rockets play a major role in space exploration. Without them, we'd still be firmly fixed on the ground. While rockets go back at least 800 years, it wasn't until the late 1600s that people began to understand the science behind them. Isaac Newton's famous three laws of motion account for rocket behavior.

First Law: An object in motion will remain in motion in a straight line and at the same speed unless acted on by an unbalanced force.

Second Law: An unbalanced force on an object will cause it to accelerate (change its speed).

Third Law: If an object is acted on by a force, it will push back in the opposite direction with an equal force.

Imagine that you are wearing roller skates and standing next to a wall. When you push against the wall, you roll backward. You pushed on the wall and the wall pushed against you. This is an example of the third law of motion. Since you could move and the wall couldn't, the unbalanced force that the wall exerted caused you to start moving, an example of the second law.

A rocket in space, or even in the atmosphere, cannot physically push against any solid object. But Newton's laws of motion still apply.

1. Fuel burns in the combustion chamber of the rocket motor. The hot gases expand and press against the sides of the combustion chamber. The sides of the combustion chamber push back against the pressure (third law).

2. Since the nozzle is open, the unbalanced force of the gas pressure accelerates the matter in the exhaust gases through the nozzle (second law).

3. The escaping exhaust gases rush out of the nozzle in one direction, causing an opposite force against the rocket (third law). This force, in turn, causes the rocket to accelerate (first and second laws).

In this lab, we're going to explore rockets using a simple physical model. As your textbook explains, rocket motors are called *reaction engines*. While we won't be burning fuel, we will do plenty of reacting!

Procedure

- Tie or tape one end of the fishing line to the back of a chair.

- Pass the free end of the line through the straw.

- Tie the other end of the line to the back of the other chair. Separate the chairs until the line is tight. Measure the distance between the two chairs to the nearest 1 cm and record the distance in meters (1 cm = 0.01 m).

Goals

After completing this lab, you will be able to

✓ demonstrate Newton's third law.

✓ explain the role Newton's laws play in rocketry.

Equipment

long balloon
drinking straw
fishing line or thread, 10 m
tape measure
stopwatch
masking tape
calculator
chairs (2)

Staying Balanced

The term *balanced* means that all forces acting on an object cancel each other out. If forces are *unbalanced*, one of the forces acting on the object is stronger than the others. Unbalanced external forces cause motion to change (acceleration).

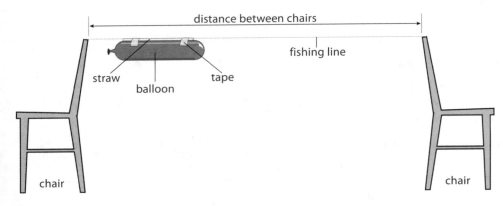

Figure 1 Balloon rocket setup

- Inflate the balloon fully. Measure its length. Release enough air so that the balloon is half the filled length. Pinch the balloon shut.

- Slide the straw back to one chair. Using two strips of masking tape, attach the straw along the length of the balloon. The balloon's opening should face toward the chair back.

- Have a partner take the stopwatch and say "3-2-1-Go!" He should start the watch as he says "Go!" Release the balloon as soon as you hear "Go!" When the balloon stops moving, your partner should stop the watch. Record the time to the nearest 0.1 s in the table below.

- Repeat the procedure two more times. Try to inflate the balloon the same amount each time.

- Average the three time values and record the result in the table.

- Repeat the procedure another three times but now *fully inflate the balloon.* Record the data in the table and calculate the average of the three values.

Half Inflation	Time (s)	Full Inflation	Time (s)
1		1	
2		2	
3		3	
Average		Average	

- Calculate and record the average speed of the half-inflated balloon by dividing the distance between the chairs by the average time. Be sure to include an appropriate speed unit after the answer.

_____

- Calculate and record the average speed of the fully inflated balloon by dividing the distance between the chairs by the average time. Be sure to include an appropriate speed unit after the answer.

_____

1. Which balloon rocket had the higher average speed?

_____

2. Describe all the factors that were different between the two balloon rockets.

name _____

_____

_____

_____

3. Which of these factors was the most important in producing the change in motion of the balloon rocket?

_____

_____

_____

4. Make a prediction as to what would happen if you could double the amount of air in the full balloon without breaking it. Explain your prediction.

_____

_____

_____

5. What other forces were acting on the balloon and straw (the moving parts of the rocket) during the run? Explain.

_____

_____

_____

6. Explain how Newton's third law makes the balloon rocket work.

_____

_____

_____

7. Would your balloon rocket work in space? Explain.

_____

_____

_____

25C Liftoff!

name_____

section_____ date_____

There's no better way to cap off your year of earth science than by launching a model rocket! For over 50 years, students have gotten a taste of the space program through this fascinating hobby. Who knows, perhaps you'll discover a new pastime that combines the best of science, adventure, and model-making skills.

Goals

After completing this lab, you will be able to
✓ build and launch a model rocket.
✓ determine the model rocket's altitude.

Procedure 1 (Building the Rocket)

- Your kit includes complete directions for building the rocket. Read the instructions carefully, making sure that you understand each step before moving on to the next. If you are ever uncertain, ask your teacher first!

- Whenever you are instructed to use glue to fasten two parts together (such as fins to the body tube), use thin layers of glue, not runny globs! It doesn't take much glue to make a strong joint. Thin layers also dry faster.

- If your model has balsa fins, sand them lightly and round their edges for the best aerodynamic performance. If you have cardboard fins, do not sand them.

- When you glue on the fins, follow the instructions carefully and make sure that they are properly aligned. Crooked fins will prevent your rocket from flying straight.

- When your rocket is finished and the glue has dried, you may want to paint it. Model spray paint is best for painting the body and nose cone. Do all painting outside and protect your clothes.

- A rolled-up sheet of newspaper thrust inside the body tube is a good way to hold the rocket while painting. It will help keep your hands clean. Apply spray paint in thin layers to keep it from running.

- After the main coat of paint has dried, you may want to do some detail painting with brushes. Your kit may also come with decals. Follow the kit instructions if you decide to use the decals.

- Let everything dry overnight before launching.

Equipment

model rocket kit
launch system (rod/pad and control box)
rocket motors and igniters
recovery wadding
clinometer from Labs 3A and 7A
white glue
model paint
hobby knife
masking tape
tape measure
protractor
centimeter ruler

Figure 1 Model rocketry is an exciting hobby!

Procedure 2 (Launching the Rocket)

- Your teacher will point you to the website of the National Association of Rocketry (NAR). Read the NAR Model Rocket Safety Code completely. Model rocketry is a safe hobby when you follow rocket safety practices. It can be very dangerous if you don't.

- Go outside to an open field well clear of buildings. Your teacher, who will be known as the Range Safety Officer (RSO), will instruct you how to set up the launching system. All

Home on the Range

In model rocket terminology, the open space where you launch rockets is called the *range*. According to NAR guidelines, the range should be at least 200 × 200 ft when used to launch rockets with B motors.

spectators not immediately concerned with the launch should stay at least 30 ft away from the pad.

- Insert recovery wadding into the top of the body tube. Make sure the shock cord is properly attached to the nose cone and body tube. Roll up the parachute or streamer according to the instructions that come with the kit. Cap the tube with the nose cone.

- Insert a model rocket motor into the bottom of the body tube with its nozzle facing out. If the rocket body has a metal clip, be sure it is secured to the bottom edge of the motor.

- Spread the wires of an igniter apart and insert the igniter tip into the motor's nozzle. Insert a plastic plug into the nozzle to retain the igniter.

- Place the model on the launch pad by sliding the launch rod through the launch lug tube. The model should rest on the metal disk at the base of the launch pad.

- Disable the control box. This is usually done by removing a safety key. Attach the clips on the control box wires to the igniter wires. Be sure that they don't touch each other or the metal disk on the launch pad.

- Alert the RSO and everyone else that you are ready to launch. Spectators should stay at least 30 ft away from the pad. The person with the launch control box should move as far away as the wires permit (at least 15 ft).

- When everyone is at a safe distance, request permission from the RSO to launch. When you receive permission, enable the control box by inserting the safety key.

- Count down as follows: "5, 4, 3, 2, 1, LAUNCH!" When you reach "LAUNCH," press the control box launch button.

- Try to keep the rocket in view so that you'll be able to see where it lands. Recover the rocket if you can do so safely.

- If the rocket fails to ignite when you press the launch button, warn all spectators that you've just had a *misfire*. Wait for instructions from the RSO. Do *not* approach the rocket without the RSO's permission.

> ### Launch?
> You may wonder why you should say LAUNCH instead of FIRE. Model rocketry enthusiasts avoid using the word *fire* for anything except actual fires. Doing this prevents confusion if a fire should happen to break out on the range.

Procedure 3 (Altitude Determination)

It's always fun to know your model rocket's maximum altitude. And you already know how to find it! Remember Labs 3A and 7A? You can use the same clinometer and procedure to determine rocket altitude.

- The observer with the clinometer should stand at least 100 m from the rocket launch pad. Having a second person read the angle is a good idea.

name _____

- When you launch the rocket, the person with the clinometer should follow its flight by watching through the straw. It goes up fast, so be ready to move!

- When the rocket reaches maximum altitude, the second person should read the angle on the protractor.

- Construct a scaled triangle just like you did in Lab 7A. Use it to determine the altitude.

- Record each rocket's altitude and see whose went the highest!

Beginning of a New Hobby?

Perhaps this lab has ignited your interest in model rocketry. If so, you couldn't have picked a better hobby! For many years, model rocket enthusiasts have been drilling holes in the sky and dreaming of space. If you wish to explore this hobby further, the following are good places to start.

- Get the book *Handbook of Model Rocketry* by G. Harry Stine, one of the founding fathers of the hobby. As of 2011, this book is in its seventh edition. Many consider it the bible of model rocketry. It is available in many libraries and is also available in e-book format.

- Spend some time on the NAR website (www.nar.org). The NAR is the organizing body of model rocketry. You should also consider joining the NAR.

- Locate a local model rocket club where you can meet other enthusiasts. Model rocket clubs also sponsor launches and competitions. Again, the NAR can direct you to the one closest to where you live.

- There are many websites maintained by companies that sell model rocket kits. Visit the EARTH SCIENCE 4th Edition Resources webpage. Under Lab Manual, Lab 25C, click on the links *ESTES*, *Quest Aerospace*, and *Aerotech* for the major suppliers of model rocket equipment.

APPENDIX

Septuagint (LXX) Texts

Genesis 11

10. And these are the generations of Shem: and Shem was an hundred years old when he begot Arphaxad, the second year after the flood.

11. And Shem lived, after he had begotten Arphaxad, five hundred years, and begot sons and daughters, and died.

12. And Arphaxad lived an hundred and thirty-five years, and begot Cainan.

13. And Arphaxad lived, after he had begotten Cainan, four hundred years, and begot sons and daughters, and died. And Cainan lived an hundred and thirty years and begot Salah; and Cainan lived, after he had begotten Salah, three hundred and thirty years, and begot sons and daughters, and died.

14. And Salah lived an hundred and thirty years, and begot Eber.

15. And Salah lived, after he had begotten Eber, three hundred and thirty years, and begot sons and daughters, and died.

16. And Eber lived an hundred and thirty-four years, and begot Peleg.

17. And Eber lived, after he had begotten Peleg, two hundred and seventy years, and begot sons and daughters, and died.

18. And Peleg lived an hundred and thirty years, and begot Reu.

19. And Peleg lived, after he had begotten Reu, two hundred and nine years, and begot sons and daughters, and died.

20. And Reu lived an hundred thirty and two years, and begot Serug.

21. And Reu lived, after he had begotten Serug, two hundred and seven years, and begot sons and daughters, and died.

22. And Serug lived an hundred and thirty years, and begot Nahor.

23. And Serug lived, after he had begotten Nahor, two hundred years, and begot sons and daughters, and died.

24. And Nahor lived an hundred and seventy-nine years, and begot Terah.

25. And Nahor lived, after he had begotten Terah, an hundred and twenty-five years, and begot sons and daughters, and died.

26. And Terah lived seventy years, and begot Abram, and Nahor, and Haran.

27. And these are the generations of Terah. Terah begot Abram, and Nahor, and Haran; and Haran begot Lot.

28. And Haran died in the presence of Terah his father, in the land in which he was born, in the country of the Chaldees.

29. And Abram and Nahor took to themselves wives, the name of the wife of Abram was Sara and the name of the wife of Nahor, Malcha, daughter of Haran, and he was the father of Malcha, the father of Jescha.

30. And Sara was barren, and did not bear children.

31. And Terah took Abram his son, and Lot the son of Haran, the son of his son, and Sara his daughter-in-law, the wife of Abram his son, and led them forth out of the land of the Chaldees, to go into the land of Chanaan [Canaan], and they came as far as Charrhan [Haran], and he dwelt there.

32. And all the days of Terah in the land of Charrhan were two hundred and five years, and Terah died in Charrhan.

Genesis 25

7. And these were the years of the days of the life of Abram as many as he lived, an hundred and seventy-five years.

8. And Abram failing died in a good old age, an old man and full of days, and was added to his people.

Genesis 35

28. And the days of Isaac which he lived were an hundred and eighty years.

29. And Isaac gave up the ghost and died, and was laid to his family, old and full of days; and Esau and Jacob his sons buried him.

Genesis 47

28. And Jacob survived seventeen years in the land of Egypt; and Jacob's days of the years of his life were an hundred and forty-seven years.

29. And the days of Israel [Jacob] drew nigh for him to die: and he called his son Joseph, and said to him, If I have found favour before thee, put thy hand under my thigh, and thou shalt execute mercy and truth toward me, so as not to bury me in Egypt.

30. But I will sleep with my fathers, and thou shalt carry me up out of Egypt, and bury me in their sepulchre. And he said, I will do according to thy word.

31. And he said, Swear to me; and he swore to him. And Israel did reverence, leaning on the top of his staff.

Genesis 50

26. And Joseph died, aged an hundred and ten years; and they prepared his corpse, and put him in a coffin in Egypt.

From *The Septuagint LXX: Greek and English* by Sir Lancelot C. L. Brenton, published by Samuel Bagster & Sons, Ltd., London, 1851. Some names have been changed to match the more familiar ones commonly found in most English Bibles.

Photograph Credits

The following agencies and individuals have furnished materials to meet the photographic needs of this textbook. We wish to express our gratitude to them for their important contribution.

Alamy
Art Resource
David Chandler Company
Donald Congdon
Esri
Fabre Minerals
Flickr
Fotolia
Getty Images
Google Earth
iStockphoto
JupiterImages
National Aeronautics and Space
    Administration (NASA)
National Oceanic and Atmospheric
    Administration (NOAA)
Don Patton
Dr. Paula Reimer
RIKEN
SuperStock
Tunç Tezel
Thinkstock
VORTEX II
Wikimedia Commons
Wikipedia

Cover
Photo and specimen: www.fabreminerals
.com

Front Matter
©Jim Arbogast/SuperStock v; Donald R.
Congdon vi, vii (top); ©iStockphoto.com/
OliverChilds vii (bottom); ©iStockphoto
.com/AWSeebaran viii (top); ©PhotoAlto/
SuperStock viii (bottom)

Chapter 1
©Alex Segre/Alamy 1; Getty Images/
iStockphoto/Thinkstock 3; Donald R.
Congdon 5 (both); ©iStockphoto.com/
compassandcamera 9 (top); ©iStockphoto
.com/Davel5957 9 (bottom)

Chapter 2
Donald R. Congdon 15-16, 19-21;
©iStockphoto.com/vandervelden 17

Chapter 3
Data SIO, NOAA, US Navy, NGA, GEBCO/
Image IBCAO/ Image ©2011 DigitalGlobe/
Image ©2011 TerraMetrics 29; Getty Images/
Axiom Photographic Agency/Marc Jackson
30 (top); Getty Images/Photographer's
Choice/Maremagnum 30 (bottom); Data
SIO, NOAA, US Navy, NGA, GEBCO 31
(top, center); William Warby/Wikipedia/

CC BY-SA 2.0 31 (bottom); ©iStockphoto
.com/Dieter Spears 32

Chapter 4
©iStockphoto.com/Igor Dmitriev 41

Chapter 5
©All Canada Photos/SuperStock 47;
©iStockphoto.com/CatherineYeulet 51;
Donald R. Congdon 56

Chapter 6
Bill Mesta/Wikimedia Commons/CC
BY-SA 3.0 61; Image IBCAO/Image ©2011
GeoEye/Data SIO, NOAA, US Navy, NGA,
GEBCO/©2011 Cnes/Spot Image 65;
Johann Dréo/Wikimedia Commons/CC
BY-SA 3.0, GFDL 66; Image IBCAO/Image
©2011 TerraMetrics /Data SIO, NOAA,
US Navy, NGA, GEBCO/©2011 Cnes/Spot
Image 67

Chapter 7
Donald R. Congdon 74

Chapter 8
Data SIO, NOAA, US Navy, NGA, GEBCO/
©2001 Cnes-Spot Image/Data ©2011
MIRC/JHA/Image ©2011 TerraMetrics
81; Data SIO, NOAA, US Navy, NGA,
GEBCO/©2001 Cnes-Spot Image/Image
IBCAO/Image ©2011 TerraMetrics 83;
Harry Glicken, USGS/CVO/Wikimedia
Commons/Public Domain 87 (top);
©iStockphoto.com/kickstand 87 (bottom)

Chapter 9
©Science Faction/SuperStock 91; Donald R.
Congdon 96

Chapter 10
EJP Photo/Flickr 99; Getty Images/Science
Photo Library/Gavin Kingcome 103 (top);
Educerva/Wikipedia/CC BY-SA 3.0, GNU
FDL 1.2 103 (bottom); ©Don Patton/www
.bible.ca 105

Chapter 11
©The Trustees of the British Museum/
Art Resource 107; Dr. Paula Reimer
(Director, Centre for Climate, the
Environment & Chronology [14CHRONO]
School of Geography, Archaeology and
Palaeoecology Queen's University Belfast
Belfast, BT7 1NN U.K.) 110; Getty Images/
DeAgostini 111

Chapter 12
Getty Images/iStockphoto/Thinkstock 115;
Donald R. Congdon 116 (all), 126 (both);
©iStockphoto.com/GordonHeeley 125

Chapter 13
Getty Images/Dorling Kindersley/Kim
Taylor and Jane Burton 129; Donald R.

Congdon 130, 134; ©2007 JupiterImages
Corporation 133

Chapter 14
©iStockphoto.com/terminator1 139

Chapter 15
©2011 Europa Technologies/©2011 Google/
Data SIO, NOAA, US Navy, NGA, GEBCO
143, 144; ©2011 Europa Technologies/©2011
Google/Image USDA Farm Service Agency/
Data SIO, NOAA, US Navy, NGA, GEBCO
145; Donald R. Congdon 148 (both)

Chapter 16
©dendron/Fotolia.com 151; ©2011 Google/
©2011 Europa Technologies/Image State of
Oregon 152; Ranveig/Wikipedia/CC BY-SA
3.0, GNU FDL 153; Wikimedia Commons/
Public Domain 154; ©Purestock/Alamy
155 (top); Donald R. Congdon 155 (bottom)

Chapter 17
NASA 159; ©Picture Contact BV/Alamy
161; Donald R. Congdon 162

Chapter 18
©Image Asset Management Ltd./
SuperStock 163; Donald R. Congdon 164,
168; Chinneeb/Wikipedia/GNU FDL, CC
BY-SA 3.0 167

Chapter 19
Donald R. Congdon 171, 175

Chapter 20
VORTEX II 179; NOAA 183

Chapter 21
©Design Pics/SuperStock 187; Courtesy
of RIKEN 190; Getty Images/Comstock
Images/Thinkstock 191

Chapter 22
Donald R. Congdon 198 (top), 202 (both);
ESO/R. Fosbury/T. Trygg/D. Rabanus/
Wikipedia/CC BY-SA 198 (bottom)

Chapter 23
Jan Sandberg/Wikipedia 209; Johannes
Kepler/Wikipedia/Public Domain 211;
Tunç Tezel 215

Chapter 24
Used With Permission of David
Chandler Company 221; Meyers Großes
Konversations-Lexikon 6/Wikipedia/
Public Domain 225

Chapter 25
Joe Schneid/Wikimedia Commons/GNU
FDL, CC BY-SA 3.0

Workpages were created using Esri software,
www.esri.com/aejee